The Deformed Transformed by Lord Byron

George Gordon Byron, 6th Baron Byron, but more commonly known as just Byron was a leading English poet in the Romantic Movement along with Keats and Shelley.

Byron was born on January 22nd, 1788. He was a great traveller across Europe, spending many years in Italy and much time in Greece. With his aristocratic indulgences, flamboyant style along with his debts, and a string of lovers he was the constant talk of society.

In 1823 he joined the Greeks in their war of Independence against the Ottoman Empire, both helping to fund and advise on the war's conduct.

It was an extraordinary adventure, even by his own standards. But, for us, it is his poetry for which he is mainly remembered even though it is difficult to see where he had time to write his works of immense beauty. But write them he did.

He died on April 19th 1824 after having contracted a cold which, on the advice of his doctors, was treated with blood-letting. This caused complications and a violent fever set in. Byron died like his fellow romantics, tragically young and on some foreign field.

Index of Contents

DRAMATIS PERSONÆ
Stranger, afterwards Cæsar
Arnold
Bourbon
Philibert
Cellini
Bertha
Olimpia
Spirits
Soldiers
Citizens of Rome
Priests

Peasants, etc

PART I

SCENE I

—A Forest.

Enter ARNOLD and his mother BERTHA.

BERTHA - Out, Hunchback!

ARNOLD - I was born so, Mother!

BERTHA - Out,
Thou incubus! Thou nightmare! Of seven sons,

The sole abortion!

ARNOLD - Would that I had been so,
And never seen the light!

BERTHA - I would so, too!
But as thou hast—hence, hence—and do thy best!
That back of thine may bear its burthen; 'tis
More high, if not so broad as that of others.

ARNOLD - It bears its burthen;—but, my heart! Will it
Sustain that which you lay upon it, Mother?
I love, or, at the least, I loved you: nothing
Save You, in nature, can love aught like me.
You nursed me—do not kill me!

BERTHA - Yes—I nursed thee,
Because thou wert my first-born, and I knew not
If there would be another unlike thee,
That monstrous sport of Nature. But get hence,
And gather wood!

ARNOLD - I will: but when I bring it,
Speak to me kindly. Though my brothers are
So beautiful and lusty, and as free
As the free chase they follow, do not spurn me:
Our milk has been the same.

BERTHA - As is the hedgehog's,
Which sucks at midnight from the wholesome dam
Of the young bull, until the milkmaid finds
The nipple, next day, sore, and udder dry.

Call not thy brothers brethren! Call me not
Mother; for if I brought thee forth, it was
As foolish hens at times hatch vipers, by
Sitting upon strange eggs. Out, urchin, out!

[Exit BERTHA.

ARNOLD - (solus).
Oh, mother!—She is gone, and I must do
Her bidding;—wearily but willingly
I would fulfil it, could I only hope
A kind word in return. What shall I do?

[ARNOLD begins to cut wood: in doing this he wounds one of his hands.

My labour for the day is over now.
Accurséd be this blood that flows so fast;

For double curses will be my meed now
At home—What home? I have no home, no kin,
No kind—not made like other creatures, or
To share their sports or pleasures. Must I bleed, too,
Like them? Oh, that each drop which falls to earth
Would rise a snake to sting them, as they have stung me!
Or that the Devil, to whom they liken me,
Would aid his likeness! If I must partake
His form, why not his power? Is it because
I have not his will too? For one kind word
From her who bore me would still reconcile me
Even to this hateful aspect. Let me wash
The wound.

[ARNOLD goes to a spring, and stoops to wash his hand: he starts back.

They are right; and Nature's mirror shows me,
What she hath made me. I will not look on it
Again, and scarce dare think on't. Hideous wretch
That I am! The very waters mock me with
My horrid shadow—like a demon placed
Deep in the fountain to scare back the cattle
From drinking therein.

[He pauses.

And shall I live on,
A burden to the earth, myself, and shame
Unto what brought me into life? Thou blood,
Which flowest so freely from a scratch, let me
Try if thou wilt not, in a fuller stream,
Pour forth my woes for ever with thyself
On earth, to which I will restore, at once,

This hateful compound of her atoms, and
Resolve back to her elements, and take
The shape of any reptile save myself,
And make a world for myriads of new worms!
This knife! now let me prove if it will sever
This withered slip of Nature's nightshade—my
Vile form—from the creation, as it hath
The green bough from the forest.

[ARNOLD places the knife in the ground, with the point upwards.

Now 'tis set,
And I can fall upon it. Yet one glance
On the fair day, which sees no foul thing like
Myself, and the sweet sun which warmed me, but
In vain. The birds—how joyously they sing!
So let them, for I would not be lamented:
But let their merriest notes be Arnold's knell;
The fallen leaves my monument; the murmur
Of the near fountain my sole elegy.
Now, knife, stand firmly, as I fain would fall!

[As he rushes to throw himself upon the knife, his eye is suddenly caught by the fountain, which seems in motion.

The fountain moves without a wind: but shall
The ripple of a spring change my resolve?
No. Yet it moves again! The waters stir,
Not as with air, but by some subterrane
And rocking Power of the internal world.
What's here? A mist! No more?—

[A cloud comes from the fountain. He stands gazing upon it: it is dispelled, and a tall black man comes towards him.

ARNOLD - What would you? Speak!
Spirit or man?

STRANGER - As man is both, why not
Say both in one?

ARNOLD - Your form is man's, and yet
You may be devil.

STRANGER - So many men are that
Which is so called or thought, that you may add me
To which you please, without much wrong to either.
But come: you wish to kill yourself;—pursue
Your purpose.

ARNOLD - You have interrupted me.

STRANGER - What is that resolution which can e'er
Be interrupted? If I be the devil
You deem, a single moment would have made you
Mine, and for ever, by your suicide;
And yet my coming saves you.

ARNOLD - I said not
You were the Demon, but that your approach
Was like one.

STRANGER - Unless you keep company
With him (and you seem scarce used to such high
Society) you can't tell how he approaches;
And for his aspect, look upon the fountain,
And then on me, and judge which of us twain
Looks likest what the boors believe to be
Their cloven-footed terror.

ARNOLD - Do you—dare you
To taunt me with my born deformity?

STRANGER - Were I to taunt a buffalo with this
Cloven foot of thine, or the swift dromedary
With thy Sublime of Humps, the animals
Would revel in the compliment. And yet
Both beings are more swift, more strong, more mighty
In action and endurance than thyself,
And all the fierce and fair of the same kind
With thee. Thy form is natural: 'twas only
Nature's mistaken largess to bestow
The gifts which are of others upon man.

ARNOLD - Give me the strength then of the buffalo's foot,
When he spurns high the dust, beholding his
Near enemy; or let me have the long
And patient swiftness of the desert-ship,
The helmless dromedary!—and I'll bear
Thy fiendish sarcasm with a saintly patience.

STRANGER - I will.

ARNOLD - (with surprise).
Thou canst?

STRANGER - Perhaps. Would you aught else?

ARNOLD - Thou mockest me.

STRANGER - Not I. Why should I mock
What all are mocking? That 's poor sport, methinks.

To talk to thee in human language (for
Thou canst not yet speak mine), the forester
Hunts not the wretched coney, but the boar,
Or wolf, or lion—leaving paltry game
To petty burghers, who leave once a year
Their walls, to fill their household cauldrons with
Such scullion prey. The meanest gibe at thee,—
Now I can mock the mightiest.

ARNOLD - Then waste not
Thy time on me: I seek thee not.

STRANGER - Your thoughts
Are not far from me. Do not send me back:
I'm not so easily recalled to do
Good service.

ARNOLD - What wilt thou do for me?

STRANGER - Change
Shapes with you, if you will, since yours so irks you;
Or form you to your wish in any shape.

ARNOLD - Oh! then you are indeed the Demon, for
Nought else would wittingly wear mine.

STRANGER - I'll show thee
The brightest which the world e'er bore, and give thee
Thy choice.

ARNOLD - On what condition?

STRANGER - There's a question!
An hour ago you would have given your soul
To look like other men, and now you pause
To wear the form of heroes.

ARNOLD - No; I will not.
I must not compromise my soul.

STRANGER - What soul,
Worth naming so, would dwell in such a carcase?

ARNOLD - 'Tis an aspiring one, whate'er the tenement
In which it is mislodged. But name your compact:
Must it be signed in blood?

STRANGER - Not in your own.

ARNOLD - Whose blood then?

STRANGER - We will talk of that hereafter.
But I'll be moderate with you, for I see
Great things within you. You shall have no bond
But your own will, no contract save your deeds.
Are you content?

ARNOLD - I take thee at thy word.

STRANGER - Now then!—

[The STRANGER approaches the fountain, and turns to ARNOLD.

A little of your blood.

ARNOLD - For what?

STRANGER - To mingle with the magic of the waters,
And make the charm effective.
ARNOLD - (holding out his wounded arm).
Take it all.

STRANGER - Not now. A few drops will suffice for this.

[The STRANGER takes some of ARNOLD'S blood in his hand, and casts it into the fountain.

Shadows of Beauty!
Shadows of Power!
Rise to your duty—
This is the hour!
Walk lovely and pliant
From the depth of this fountain,
As the cloud-shapen giant
Bestrides the Hartz Mountain.
Come as ye were,
That our eyes may behold
The model in air
Of the form I will mould,
Bright as the Iris
When ether is spanned;—
Such his desire is,

[Pointing to ARNOLD.

Such my command!
Demons heroic—
Demons who wore
The form of the Stoic
Or sophist of yore—

Or the shape of each victor—

From Macedon's boy,
To each high Roman's picture,
Who breathed to destroy—
Shadows of Beauty!
Shadows of Power!
Up to your duty—
This is the hour!

[Various phantoms arise from the waters, and pass in succession before the STRANGER and ARNOLD.

ARNOLD - What do I see?

STRANGER - The black-eyed Roman, with
The eagle's beak between those eyes which ne'er
Beheld a conqueror, or looked along
The land he made not Rome's, while Rome became
His, and all theirs who heired his very name.

ARNOLD - The phantom 's bald; my quest is beauty. Could I
Inherit but his fame with his defects!

STRANGER - His brow was girt with laurels more than hairs.
You see his aspect—choose it, or reject.
I can but promise you his form; his fame
Must be long sought and fought for.

ARNOLD - I will fight, too,
But not as a mock Cæsar. Let him pass:
His aspect may be fair, but suits me not.

STRANGER - Then you are far more difficult to please
Than Cato's sister, or than Brutus's mother,
Or Cleopatra at sixteen—an age
When love is not less in the eye than heart.
But be it so! Shadow, pass on!

[The PHANTOM of Julius Cæsar disappears.

ARNOLD - And can it
Be, that the man who shook the earth is gone,
And left no footstep?

STRANGER - There you err. His substance
Left graves enough, and woes enough, and fame
More than enough to track his memory;
But for his shadow—'tis no more than yours,
Except a little longer and less crooked
I' the sun. Behold another!

[A second PHANTOM passes.

ARNOLD - Who is he?

STRANGER - He was the fairest and the bravest of
Athenians. Look upon him well.

ARNOLD - He is
More lovely than the last. How beautiful!

STRANGER - Such was the curled son of Clinias;—wouldst thou
Invest thee with his form?

ARNOLD - Would that I had
Been born with it! But since I may choose further,
I will look further.
[The shade of Alcibiades disappears.

STRANGER - Lo! behold again!

ARNOLD - What! that low, swarthy, short-nosed, round-eyed satyr,
With the wide nostrils and Silenus' aspect,
The splay feet and low stature! I had better
Remain that which I am.

STRANGER -
And yet he was
The earth's perfection of all mental beauty,
And personification of all virtue.
But you reject him?

ARNOLD - If his form could bring me
That which redeemed it—no.

STRANGER - I have no power
To promise that; but you may try, and find it
Easier in such a form—or in your own.

ARNOLD - No. I was not born for philosophy,
Though I have that about me which has need on't.
Let him fleet on.

STRANGER - Be air, thou Hemlock-drinker!

[The SHADOW of Socrates disappears: another rises.

ARNOLD - What's here? whose broad brow and whose curly beard
And manly aspect look like Hercules,
Save that his jocund eye hath more of Bacchus
Than the sad purger of the infernal world,
Leaning dejected on his club of conquest,
As if he knew the worthlessness of those
For whom he had fought.

STRANGER - It was the man who lost
The ancient world for love.

ARNOLD - I cannot blame him,
Since I have risked my soul because I find not
That which he exchanged the earth for.

STRANGER - Since so far
You seem congenial, will you wear his features?

ARNOLD - No. As you leave me choice, I am difficult.
If but to see the heroes I should ne'er
Have seen else, on this side of the dim shore,
Whence they float back before us.

STRANGER - Hence, Triumvir,
Thy Cleopatra 's waiting.

[The shade of Antony disappears: another rises.

ARNOLD - Who is this?
Who truly looketh like a demigod,
Blooming and bright, with golden hair, and stature,
If not more high than mortal, yet immortal
In all that nameless bearing of his limbs,
Which he wears as the Sun his rays—a something
Which shines from him, and yet is but the flashing
Emanation of a thing more glorious still.
Was he e'er human only?

STRANGER - Let the earth speak,
If there be atoms of him left, or even
Of the more solid gold that formed his urn.

ARNOLD - Who was this glory of mankind?

STRANGER - The shame
Of Greece in peace, her thunderbolt in war—
Demetrius the Macedonian, and
Taker of cities.

ARNOLD - Yet one shadow more.

STRANGER - (addressing the shadow).
Get thee to Lamia's lap!

[The shade of Demetrius Poliorcetes vanishes: another rises.

I'll fit you still,
Fear not, my Hunchback: if the shadows of

That which existed please not your nice taste,
I'll animate the ideal marble, till
Your soul be reconciled to her new garment.

ARNOLD - Content! I will fix here.

STRANGER - I must commend
Your choice. The godlike son of the sea-goddess,
The unshorn boy of Peleus, with his locks
As beautiful and clear as the amber waves
Of rich Pactolus, rolled o'er sands of gold,
Softened by intervening crystal, and
Rippled like flowing waters by the wind,

All vowed to Sperchius as they were—behold them!
And him—as he stood by Polixena,
With sanctioned and with softened love, before
The altar, gazing on his Trojan bride,
With some remorse within for Hector slain
And Priam weeping, mingled with deep passion
For the sweet downcast virgin, whose young hand
Trembled in his who slew her brother. So
He stood i' the temple! Look upon him as
Greece looked her last upon her best, the instant
Ere Paris' arrow flew.

ARNOLD - I gaze upon him
As if I were his soul, whose form shall soon
Envelope mine.

STRANGER - You have done well. The greatest
Deformity should only barter with
The extremest beauty—if the proverb 's true
Of mortals, that Extremes meet.

ARNOLD - Come! Be quick!
I am impatient.

STRANGER - As a youthful beauty
Before her glass. You both see what is not,
But dream it is what must be.

ARNOLD - Must I wait?

STRANGER - No; that were a pity. But a word or two:
His stature is twelve cubits; would you so far
Outstep these times, and be a Titan? Or
(To talk canonically) wax a son
Of Anak?

ARNOLD - Why not?

STRANGER - Glorious ambition!
I love thee most in dwarfs! A mortal of
Philistine stature would have gladly pared
His own Goliath down to a slight David:
But thou, my manikin, wouldst soar a show
Rather than hero. Thou shalt be indulged,

If such be thy desire; and, yet, by being
A little less removed from present men
In figure, thou canst sway them more; for all
Would rise against thee now, as if to hunt
A new-found Mammoth; and their curséd engines,
Their culverins, and so forth, would find way
Through our friend's armour there, with greater ease
Than the Adulterer's arrow through his heel
Which Thetis had forgotten to baptize
In Styx.

ARNOLD - Then let it be as thou deem'st best.

STRANGER - Thou shalt be beauteous as the thing thou seest,
And strong as what it was, and—

ARNOLD - I ask not
For Valour, since Deformity is daring.
It is its essence to o'ertake mankind
By heart and soul, and make itself the equal—
Aye, the superior of the rest. There is
A spur in its halt movements, to become
All that the others cannot, in such things
As still are free to both, to compensate
For stepdame Nature's avarice at first.
They woo with fearless deeds the smiles of fortune,
And oft, like Timour the lame Tartar, win them.

STRANGER - Well spoken! And thou doubtless wilt remain
Formed as thou art. I may dismiss the mould
Of shadow, which must turn to flesh, to incase
This daring soul, which could achieve no less
Without it.

ARNOLD - Had no power presented me
The possibility of change, I would
Have done the best which spirit may to make
Its way with all Deformity's dull, deadly,
Discouraging weight upon me, like a mountain,
In feeling, on my heart as on my shoulders—
A hateful and unsightly molehill to
The eyes of happier men. I would have looked
On Beauty in that sex which is the type

Of all we know or dream of beautiful,
Beyond the world they brighten, with a sigh—
Not of love, but despair; nor sought to win,
Though to a heart all love, what could not love me
In turn, because of this vile crookéd clog,
Which makes me lonely. Nay, I could have borne
It all, had not my mother spurned me from her.
The she-bear licks her cubs into a sort
Of shape;—my Dam beheld my shape was hopeless.
Had she exposed me, like the Spartan, ere
I knew the passionate part of life, I had
Been a clod of the valley,—happier nothing
Than what I am. But even thus—the lowest,
Ugliest, and meanest of mankind—what courage
And perseverance could have done, perchance
Had made me something—as it has made heroes
Of the same mould as mine. You lately saw me
Master of my own life, and quick to quit it;
And he who is so is the master of
Whatever dreads to die.

STRANGER - Decide between
What you have been, or will be.

ARNOLD - I have done so.
You have opened brighter prospects to my eyes,
And sweeter to my heart. As I am now,
I might be feared—admired—respected—loved
Of all save those next to me, of whom I
Would be belovéd. As thou showest me
A choice of forms, I take the one I view.
Haste! haste!

STRANGER - And what shall I wear?

ARNOLD - Surely, he
Who can command all forms will choose the highest,
Something superior even to that which was
Pelides now before us. Perhaps his
Who slew him, that of Paris: or—still higher—
The Poet's God, clothed in such limbs as are
Themselves a poetry.

STRANGER - Less will content me;
For I, too, love a change.

ARNOLD - Your aspect is
Dusky, but not uncomely.

STRANGER - If I chose,
I might be whiter; but I have a penchant

For black—it is so honest, and, besides,
Can neither blush with shame nor pale with fear;
But I have worn it long enough of late,
And now I'll take your figure.

ARNOLD - Mine!

STRANGER - Yes. You
Shall change with Thetis' son, and I with Bertha,
Your mother's offspring. People have their tastes;
You have yours—I mine.

ARNOLD - Despatch! despatch!

STRANGER - Even so.

[The STRANGER takes some earth and moulds it along the turf, and then addresses the phantom of Achilles.

Beautiful shadow
Of Thetis's boy!
Who sleeps in the meadow
Whose grass grows o'er Troy:
From the red earth, like Adam,
Thy likeness I shape,
As the Being who made him,
Whose actions I ape.
Thou Clay, be all glowing,
Till the Rose in his cheek
Be as fair as, when blowing,
It wears its first streak!

Ye Violets, I scatter,
Now turn into eyes!
And thou, sunshiny Water,
Of blood take the guise!
Let these Hyacinth boughs
Be his long flowing hair,
And wave o'er his brows,
As thou wavest in air!
Let his heart be this marble
I tear from the rock!
But his voice as the warble
Of birds on yon oak!
Let his flesh be the purest
Of mould, in which grew
The Lily-root surest,
And drank the best dew!
Let his limbs be the lightest
Which clay can compound,
And his aspect the brightest

On earth to be found!
Elements, near me,
Be mingled and stirred,
Know me, and hear me,
And leap to my word!
Sunbeams, awaken
This earth's animation!
'Tis done! He hath taken
His stand in creation!

[ARNOLD falls senseless; his soul passes into the shape of Achilles, which rises from the ground; while the PHANTOM has disappeared, part by part, as the figure was formed from the earth.

ARNOLD - (in his new form).
I love, and I shall be beloved! Oh, life!
At last I feel thee! Glorious Spirit!

STRANGER - Stop!
What shall become of your abandoned garment,
Yon hump, and lump, and clod of ugliness,
Which late you wore, or were?

ARNOLD - Who cares? Let wolves
And vultures take it, if they will.

STRANGER - And if
They do, and are not scared by it, you'll say
It must be peace-time, and no better fare
Abroad i' the fields.

ARNOLD - Let us but leave it there;
No matter what becomes on't.

STRANGER - That's ungracious;
If not ungrateful. Whatsoe'er it be,
It hath sustained your soul full many a day.

ARNOLD - Aye, as the dunghill may conceal a gem
Which is now set in gold, as jewels should be.

STRANGER - But if I give another form, it must be
By fair exchange, not robbery. For they
Who make men without women's aid have long
Had patents for the same, and do not love
Your Interlopers. The Devil may take men,
Not make them,—though he reap the benefit
Of the original workmanship:—and therefore
Some one must be found to assume the shape
You have quitted.

ARNOLD - Who would do so?

STRANGER - That I know not,
And therefore I must.

ARNOLD - You!

STRANGER - I said it ere
You inhabited your present dome of beauty.

ARNOLD - True. I forget all things in the new joy
Of this immortal change.

STRANGER - In a few moments
I will be as you were, and you shall see
Yourself for ever by you, as your shadow.

ARNOLD - I would be spared this.

STRANGER - But it cannot be.
What! shrink already, being what you are,
From seeing what you were?

ARNOLD - Do as thou wilt.

STRANGER - (to the late form of ARNOLD, extended on the earth).
Clay! not dead, but soul-less!
Though no man would choose thee,
An Immortal no less
Deigns not to refuse thee.
Clay thou art; and unto spirit
All clay is of equal merit.
Fire! without which nought can live;
Fire! but in which nought can live,
Save the fabled salamander,
Or immortal souls, which wander,
Praying what doth not forgive,
Howling for a drop of water,
Burning in a quenchless lot:
Fire! the only element
Where nor fish, beast, bird, nor worm,
Save the Worm which dieth not,
Can preserve a moment's form,
But must with thyself be blent:
Fire! man's safeguard and his slaughter:
Fire! Creation's first-born Daughter,
And Destruction's threatened Son,
When Heaven with the world hath done:
Fire! assist me to renew
Life in what lies in my view
Stiff and cold!
His resurrection rests with me and you!

One little, marshy spark of flame—
And he again shall seem the same;
But I his Spirit's place shall hold!

[An ignis-fatuus flits through the wood and rests on the brow of the body. The STRANGER disappears: the body rises.

ARNOLD - (in his new form).
Oh! horrible!

STRANGER - (in ARNOLD'S late shape).
What! tremblest thou?

ARNOLD - Not so—
I merely shudder. Where is fled the shape
Thou lately worest?

STRANGER - To the world of shadows.
But let us thread the present. Whither wilt thou?

ARNOLD - Must thou be my companion?

STRANGER - Wherefore not?
Your betters keep worse company.

ARNOLD - My betters!

STRANGER - Oh! you wax proud, I see, of your new form:
I'm glad of that. Ungrateful too! That 's well;
You improve apace;—two changes in an instant,
And you are old in the World's ways already.
But bear with me: indeed you'll find me useful
Upon your pilgrimage. But come, pronounce
Where shall we now be errant?

ARNOLD - Where the World
Is thickest, that I may behold it in
Its workings.

STRANGER - That 's to say, where there is War
And Woman in activity. Let's see!
Spain—Italy—the new Atlantic world—
Afric with all its Moors. In very truth,
There i small choice: the whole race are just now
Tugging as usual at each other's hearts.

ARNOLD - I have heard great things of Rome.

STRANGER - A goodly choice—
And scarce a better to be found on earth,
Since Sodom was put out. The field is wide too;

For now the Frank, and Hun, and Spanish scion
Of the old Vandals, are at play along
The sunny shores of the World's garden.

ARNOLD -
How
Shall we proceed?

STRANGER - Like gallants, on good coursers.
What, ho! my chargers! Never yet were better,
Since Phaeton was upset into the Po.
Our pages too!

Enter two PAGES, with four coal-black horses.

ARNOLD - A noble sight!

STRANGER - And of
A nobler breed. Match me in Barbary,
Or your Kochlini race of Araby,
With these!

ARNOLD - The mighty steam, which volumes high
From their proud nostrils, burns the very air;
And sparks of flame, like dancing fire-flies wheel
Around their manes, as common insects swarm
Round common steeds towards sunset.

STRANGER - Mount, my lord:
They and I are your servitors.

ARNOLD - And these
Our dark-eyed pages—what may be their names?

STRANGER - You shall baptize them.

ARNOLD - What! in holy water?

STRANGER - Why not? The deeper sinner, better saint.

ARNOLD - They are beautiful, and cannot, sure, be demons.

STRANGER - True; the devil's always ugly: and your beauty
Is never diabolical.

ARNOLD - I'll call him
Who bears the golden horn, and wears such bright
And blooming aspect, Huon; for he looks
Like to the lovely boy lost in the forest,
And never found till now. And for the other
And darker, and more thoughtful, who smiles not,

But looks as serious though serene as night,
He shall be Memnon, from the Ethiop king
Whose statue turns a harper once a day.
And you?

STRANGER - I have ten thousand names, and twice
As many attributes; but as I wear
A human shape, will take a human name.

ARNOLD - More human than the shape (though it was mine once)
I trust.

STRANGER - Then call me Cæsar.

ARNOLD - Why, that name
Belongs to Empire, and has been but borne
By the World's lords.

STRANGER - And therefore fittest for
The Devil in disguise—since so you deem me,
Unless you call me Pope instead.

ARNOLD - Well, then,
Cæsar thou shalt be. For myself, my name
Shall be plain Arnold still.

CÆSAR - We'll add a title—
"Count Arnold:" it hath no ungracious sound,
And will look well upon a billet-doux.

ARNOLD - Or in an order for a battle-field.

CÆSAR - (sings).
To horse! to horse! my coal-black steed
Paws the ground and snuffs the air!
There 's not a foal of Arab's breed
More knows whom he must bear;
On the hill he will not tire,
Swifter as it waxes higher;
In the marsh he will not slacken,
On the plain be overtaken;
In the wave he will not sink,
Nor pause at the brook's side to drink;
In the race he will not pant,
In the combat he'll not faint;
On the stones he will not stumble,
Time nor toil shall make him humble;
In the stall he will not stiffen,
But be wingèd as a Griffin,
Only flying with his feet:
And will not such a voyage be sweet?

Merrily! merrily! never unsound,
Shall our bonny black horses skim over the ground!
From the Alps to the Caucasus, ride we, or fly!
For we'll leave them behind in the glance of an eye.

[They mount their horses, and disappear.

SCENE II

—A Camp before the walls of Rome.

ARNOLD and CÆSAR.

CÆSAR - You are well entered now.

ARNOLD - Aye; but my path
Has been o'er carcasses: mine eyes are full
Of blood.

CÆSAR - Then wipe them, and see clearly. Why!
Thou art a conqueror; the chosen knight
And free companion of the gallant Bourbon,
Late constable of France; and now to be
Lord of the city which hath been Earth's Lord
Under its emperors, and—changing sex,
Not sceptre, an Hermaphrodite of Empire—
Lady of the old world.

ARNOLD - How old? What! are there
New worlds?

CÆSAR - To you. You'll find there are such shortly,
By its rich harvests, new disease, and gold;
From one half of the world named a whole new one,
Because you know no better than the dull
And dubious notice of your eyes and ears.

ARNOLD - I'll trust them.

CÆSAR - Do! They will deceive you sweetly,
And that is better than the bitter truth.

ARNOLD - Dog!

CÆSAR - Man!

ARNOLD - Devil!

CÆSAR - Your obedient humble servant.

ARNOLD - Say master rather. Thou hast lured me on,
Through scenes of blood and lust, till I am here.

CÆSAR - And where wouldst thou be?

ARNOLD -
Oh, at peace—in peace!

CÆSAR - And where is that which is so? From the star
To the winding worm, all life is motion; and
In life commotion is the extremest point
Of life. The planet wheels till it becomes
A comet, and destroying as it sweeps
The stars, goes out. The poor worm winds its way,
Living upon the death of other things,
But still, like them, must live and die, the subject
Of something which has made it live and die.
You must obey what all obey, the rule
Of fixed Necessity: against her edict
Rebellion prospers not.

ARNOLD -
And when it prospers—

CÆSAR - 'Tis no rebellion.

ARNOLD - Will it prosper now?

CÆSAR - The Bourbon hath given orders for the assault,
And by the dawn there will be work.

ARNOLD - Alas!
And shall the city yield? I see the giant
Abode of the true God, and his true saint,
Saint Peter, rear its dome and cross into
That sky whence Christ ascended from the cross,
Which his blood made a badge of glory and
Of joy (as once of torture unto him),—
God and God's Son, man's sole and only refuge!

CÆSAR - 'Tis there, and shall be.

ARNOLD - What?

CÆSAR - The Crucifix
Above, and many altar shrines below.
Also some culverins upon the walls,
And harquebusses, and what not; besides
The men who are to kindle them to death
Of other men.

ARNOLD - And those scarce mortal arches,
Pile above pile of everlasting wall,
The theatre where Emperors and their subjects
(Those subjects Romans) stood at gaze upon
The battles of the monarchs of the wild
And wood—the lion and his tusky rebels
Of the then untamed desert, brought to joust
In the arena—as right well they might,
When they had left no human foe unconquered—
Made even the forest pay its tribute of
Life to their amphitheatre, as well
As Dacia men to die the eternal death
For a sole instant's pastime, and "Pass on
To a new gladiator!"—Must it fall?

CÆSAR -
The city, or the amphitheatre?
The church, or one, or all? for you confound
Both them and me.

ARNOLD - To-morrow sounds the assault
With the first cock-crow.

CÆSAR - Which, if it end with
The evening's first nightingale, will be
Something new in the annals of great sieges;
For men must have their prey after long toil.

ARNOLD - The sun goes down as calmly, and perhaps
More beautifully, than he did on Rome
On the day Remus leapt her wall.

CÆSAR - I saw him.

ARNOLD - You!

CÆSAR - Yes, Sir! You forget I am or was
Spirit, till I took up with your cast shape,
And a worse name. I'm Cæsar and a hunch-back
Now. Well! the first of Cæsars was a bald-head,
And loved his laurels better as a wig
(So history says) than as a glory. Thus
The world runs on, but we'll be merry still.
I saw your Romulus (simple as I am)
Slay his own twin, quick-born of the same womb,
Because he leapt a ditch ('twas then no wall,
Whate'er it now be); and Rome's earliest cement
Was brother's blood; and if its native blood
Be spilt till the choked Tiber be as red
As e'er 'twas yellow, it will never wear

The deep hue of the Ocean and the Earth,
Which the great robber sons of fratricide
Have made their never-ceasing scene of slaughter,
For ages.

ARNOLD - But what have these done, their far
Remote descendants, who have lived in peace,
The peace of Heaven, and in her sunshine of
Piety?

CÆSAR - And what had they done, whom the old
Romans o'erswept?—Hark!

ARNOLD - They are soldiers singing
A reckless roundelay, upon the eve
Of many deaths, it may be of their own.

CÆSAR - And why should they not sing as well as swans?
They are black ones, to be sure.

ARNOLD - So, you are learned,
I see, too?

CÆSAR - In my grammar, certes. I
Was educated for a monk of all times,
And once I was well versed in the forgotten
Etruscan letters, and—were I so minded—
Could make their hieroglyphics plainer than
Your alphabet.

ARNOLD - And wherefore do you not?

CÆSAR - It answers better to resolve the alphabet
Back into hieroglyphics. Like your statesman,
And prophet, pontiff, doctor, alchymist,
Philosopher, and what not, they have built
More Babels, without new dispersion, than
The stammering young ones of the flood's dull ooze,
Who failed and fled each other. Why? why, marry,
Because no man could understand his neighbour.
They are wiser now, and will not separate
For nonsense. Nay, it is their brotherhood,
Their Shibboleth—their Koran—Talmud—their
Cabala—their best brick-work, wherewithal
They build more—

ARNOLD - (interrupting him).
Oh, thou everlasting sneerer!
Be silent! How the soldier's rough strain seems
Softened by distance to a hymn-like cadence!
Listen!

CÆSAR - Yes. I have heard the angels sing.

ARNOLD - And demons howl.

CÆSAR - And man, too. Let us listen:
I love all music.
Song of the Soldiers within.
The black bands came over
The Alps and their snow;
With Bourbon, the rover,
They passed the broad Po.
We have beaten all foemen,
We have captured a King,
We have turned back on no men,
And so let us sing!
Here's the Bourbon for ever!
Though penniless all,
We'll have one more endeavour
At yonder old wall.
With the Bourbon we'll gather
At day-dawn before
The gates, and together
Or break or climb o'er
The wall: on the ladder,
As mounts each firm foot,
Our shout shall grow gladder,
And Death only be mute.
With the Bourbon we'll mount o'er
The walls of old Rome,
And who then shall count o'er
The spoils of each dome?

Up! up with the Lily!
And down with the Keys!
In old Rome, the seven-hilly,
We'll revel at ease.
Her streets shall be gory,
Her Tiber all red,
And her temples so hoary
Shall clang with our tread.
Oh, the Bourbon! the Bourbon!
The Bourbon for aye!
Of our song bear the burden!
And fire, fire away!
With Spain for the vanguard,
Our varied host comes;
And next to the Spaniard
Beat Germany's drums;
And Italy's lances
Are couched at their mother;

But our leader from France is,
Who warred with his brother.
Oh, the Bourbon! the Bourbon!
Sans country or home,
We'll follow the Bourbon,
To plunder old Rome.

CÆSAR -
An indifferent song
For those within the walls, methinks, to hear.

ARNOLD - Yes, if they keep to their chorus. But here comes
The general with his chiefs and men of trust.
A goodly rebel.

Enter the Constable BOURBON "cum suis," etc., etc.

PHILIBERT - How now, noble Prince,
You are not cheerful?

BOURBON - Why should I be so?

PHILIBERT - Upon the eve of conquest, such as ours,
Most men would be so.

BOURBON - If I were secure!

PHILIBERT - Doubt not our soldiers. Were the walls of adamant,
They'd crack them. Hunger is a sharp artillery.

BOURBON - That they will falter is my least of fears.
That they will be repulsed, with Bourbon for
Their chief, and all their kindled appetites
To marshal them on—were those hoary walls
Mountains, and those who guard them like the gods
Of the old fables, I would trust my Titans;—
But now—

PHILIBERT - They are but men who war with mortals.

BOURBON - True: but those walls have girded in great ages,
And sent forth mighty spirits. The past earth
And present phantom of imperious Rome
Is peopled with those warriors; and methinks
They flit along the eternal City's rampart,
And stretch their glorious, gory, shadowy hands,
And beckon me away!

PHILIBERT - So let them! Wilt thou
Turn back from shadowy menaces of shadows?

BOURBON - They do not menace me. I could have faced,
Methinks, a Sylla's menace; but they clasp,
And raise, and wring their dim and deathlike hands,
And with their thin aspen faces and fixed eyes
Fascinate mine. Look there!

PHILIBERT - I look upon
A lofty battlement.

BOURBON - And there!

PHILIBERT - Not even
A guard in sight; they wisely keep below,
Sheltered by the grey parapet from some
Stray bullet of our lansquenets, who might
Practise in the cool twilight.

BOURBON - You are blind.

PHILIBERT - If seeing nothing more than may be seen
Be so.

BOURBON - A thousand years have manned the walls
With all their heroes,—the last Cato stands
And tears his bowels, rather than survive
The liberty of that I would enslave.
And the first Cæsar with his triumphs flits
From battlement to battlement.

PHILIBERT - Then conquer
The walls for which he conquered and be greater!

BOURBON - True: so I will, or perish.

PHILIBERT - You can not.
In such an enterprise to die is rather
The dawn of an eternal day, than death.

[Count ARNOLD and CÆSAR advanoe.

CÆSAR - And the mere men—do they, too, sweat beneath
The noon of this same ever-scorching glory?

BOURBON - Ah!
Welcome the bitter Hunchback! and his master,
The beauty of our host, and brave as beauteous,
And generous as lovely. We shall find
Work for you both ere morning.

CÆSAR - You will find,
So please your Highness, no less for yourself.

BOURBON - And if I do, there will not be a labourer
More forward, Hunchback!

CÆSAR - You may well say so,
For you have seen that back—as general,
Placed in the rear in action—but your foes
Have never seen it.

BOURBON - That 's a fair retort,
For I provoked it:—but the Bourbon's breast
Has been, and ever shall be, far advanced
In danger's face as yours, were you the devil.

CÆSAR - And if I were, I might have saved myself
The toil of coming here.

PHILIBERT - Why so?

CÆSAR - One half
Of your brave bands of their own bold accord
Will go to him, the other half be sent,
More swiftly, not less surely.

BOURBON - Arnold, your
Slight crooked friend's as snake-like in his words
As his deeds.

CÆSAR - Your Highness much mistakes me.
The first snake was a flatterer—I am none;
And for my deeds, I only sting when stung.

BOURBON - You are brave, and that's enough for me; and quick
In speech as sharp in action—and that's more.
I am not alone the soldier, but the soldiers'
Comrade.

CÆSAR - They are but bad company, your Highness;
And worse even for their friends than foes, as being
More permanent acquaintance.

PHILIBERT - How now, fellow!
Thou waxest insolent, beyond the privilege
Of a buffoon.

CÆSAR - You mean I speak the truth.
I'll lie—it is as easy: then you'll praise me
For calling you a hero.

BOURBON - Philibert!
Let him alone; he's brave, and ever has

Been first, with that swart face and mountain shoulder,
In field or storm, and patient in starvation;
And for his tongue, the camp is full of licence,
And the sharp stinging of a lively rogue
Is, to my mind, far preferable to
The gross, dull, heavy, gloomy execration
Of a mere famished sullen grumbling slave,
Whom nothing can convince save a full meal,
And wine, and sleep, and a few Maravedis,
With which he deems him rich.

CÆSAR - It would be well
If the earth's princes asked no more.

BOURBON - Be silent!

CÆSAR - Aye, but not idle. Work yourself with words!
You have few to speak.

PHILIBERT - What means the audacious prater?

CÆSAR - To prate, like other prophets.

BOURBON - Philibert!
Why will you vex him? Have we not enough
To think on? Arnold! I will lead the attack
To-morrow.

ARNOLD - I have heard as much, my Lord.

BOURBON - And you will follow?

ARNOLD - Since I must not lead.

BOURBON - 'Tis necessary for the further daring
Of our too needy army, that their chief
Plant the first foot upon the foremost ladder's
First step.

CÆSAR - Upon its topmost, let us hope:
So shall he have his full deserts.

BOURBON - The world's
Great capital perchance is ours to-morrow.
Through every change the seven-hilled city hath
Retained her sway o'er nations, and the Cæsars
But yielded to the Alarics, the Alarics
Unto the pontiffs. Roman, Goth, or priest,
Still the world's masters! Civilised, barbarian,
Or saintly, still the walls of Romulus
Have been the circus of an Empire. Well!

'Twas their turn—now 'tis ours; and let us hope
That we will fight as well, and rule much better.

CÆSAR - No doubt, the camp's the school of civic rights.
What would you make of Rome?

BOURBON - That which it was.

CÆSAR - In Alaric's time?

BOURBON - No, slave! in the first Cæsar's,
Whose name you bear like other curs—

CÆSAR - And kings!
'Tis a great name for blood-hounds.

BOURBON - There's a demon
In that fierce rattlesnake thy tongue. Wilt never
Be serious?

CÆSAR - On the eve of battle, no;—
That were not soldier-like. 'Tis for the general
To be more pensive: we adventurers
Must be more cheerful. Wherefore should we think?
Our tutelar Deity, in a leader's shape,
Takes care of us. Keep thought aloof from hosts!
If the knaves take to thinking, you will have
To crack those walls alone.

BOURBON - You may sneer, since
'Tis lucky for you that you fight no worse for 't.

CÆSAR - I thank you for the freedom; 'tis the only
Pay I have taken in your Highness' service.

BOURBON - Well, sir, to-morrow you shall pay yourself.
Look on those towers; they hold my treasury:
But, Philibert, we'll in to council. Arnold,
We would request your presence.

ARNOLD - Prince! my service
Is yours, as in the field.

BOURBON - In both we prize it,
And yours will be a post of trust at daybreak.

CÆSAR - And mine?

BOURBON - To follow glory with the Bourbon.
Good night!

ARNOLD - (to CÆSAR).
Prepare our armour for the assault,
And wait within my tent.

[Exeunt BOURBON, ARNOLD, PHILIBERT, etc.

CÆSAR - (solus).
Within thy tent!
Think'st thou that I pass from thee with my presence?
Or that this crooked coffer, which contained
Thy principle of life, is aught to me
Except a mask? And these are men, forsooth!
Heroes and chiefs, the flower of Adam's bastards!
This is the consequence of giving matter
The power of thought. It is a stubborn substance,
And thinks chaotically, as it acts,
Ever relapsing into its first elements.
Well! I must play with these poor puppets: 'tis
The Spirit's pastime in his idler hours.
When I grow weary of it, I have business
Amongst the stars, which these poor creatures deem
Were made for them to look at. 'Twere a jest now
To bring one down amongst them, and set fire
Unto their anthill: how the pismires then

Would scamper o'er the scalding soil, and, ceasing
From tearing down each other's nests, pipe forth
One universal orison! ha! ha!

[Exit CÆSAR.

PART II

SCENE I

—Before the walls of Rome.—The Assault: the Army in motion, with ladders to scale the walls;
BOURBON with a white scarf over his armour, foremost.

Chorus of Spirits in the air.
I.
'Tis the morn, but dim and dark.
Whither flies the silent lark?
Whither shrinks the clouded sun?
Is the day indeed begun?
Nature's eye is melancholy
O'er the city high and holy:
But without there is a din
Should arouse the saints within,
And revive the heroic ashes

Round which yellow Tiber dashes.
Oh, ye seven hills! awaken,
Ere your very base be shaken!

II.
Hearken to the steady stamp!
Mars is in their every tramp!
Not a step is out of tune,
As the tides obey the moon!
On they march, though to self-slaughter,
Regular as rolling water,
Whose high-waves o'ersweep the border
Of huge moles, but keep their order,
Breaking only rank by rank.
Hearken to the armour's clank!
Look down o'er each frowning warrior,
How he glares upon the barrier:
Look on each step of each ladder,
As the stripes that streak an adder.

III.
Look upon the bristling wall,
Manned without an interval!
Round and round, and tier on tier,
Cannon's black mouth, shining spear,
Lit match, bell-mouthed Musquetoon,
Gaping to be murderous soon;
All the warlike gear of old,
Mixed with what we now behold,
In this strife 'twixt old and new,
Gather like a locusts' crew.
Shade of Remus! 'tis a time
Awful as thy brother's crime!
Christians war against Christ's shrine:—
Must its lot be like to thine?

IV.
Near—and near—and nearer still,
As the Earthquake saps the hill,
First with trembling, hollow motion,
Like a scarce awakened ocean,
Then with stronger shock and louder,
Till the rocks are crushed to powder,—
Onward sweeps the rolling host!
Heroes of the immortal boast!
Mighty Chiefs! eternal shadows!
First flowers of the bloody meadows

Which encompass Rome, the mother
Of a people without brother!
Will you sleep when nations' quarrels

Plough the root up of your laurels?
Ye who weep o'er Carthage burning,
Weep not—strike! for Rome is mourning!

V.
Onward sweep the varied nations!
Famine long hath dealt their rations.
To the wall, with hate and hunger,
Numerous as wolves, and stronger,
On they sweep. Oh, glorious City!
Must thou be a theme for pity?
Fight, like your first sire, each Roman!
Alaric was a gentle foeman,
Matched with Bourbon's black banditti!
Rouse thee, thou eternal City;
Rouse thee! Rather give the torch
With thine own hand to thy porch,
Than behold such hosts pollute
Your worst dwelling with their foot.

VI.
Ah! behold yon bleeding spectre!
Ilion's children find no Hector;
Priam's offspring loved their brother;
Rome's great sire forgot his mother,
When he slew his gallant twin,
With inexpiable sin.
See the giant shadow stride
O'er the ramparts high and wide!
When the first o'erleapt thy wall,
Its foundation mourned thy fall.
Now, though towering like a Babel,
Who to stop his steps are able?
Stalking o'er thy highest dome,
Remus claims his vengeance, Rome!

VII.
Now they reach thee in their anger:
Fire and smoke and hellish clangour
Are around thee, thou world's wonder!
Death is in thy walls and under.
Now the meeting steel first clashes,
Downward then the ladder crashes,
With its iron load all gleaming,
Lying at its foot blaspheming!
Up again! for every warrior
Slain, another climbs the barrier.
Thicker grows the strife: thy ditches
Europe's mingling gore enriches.
Rome! although thy wall may perish,
Such manure thy fields will cherish,

Making gay the harvest-home;
But thy hearths, alas! oh, Rome!—
Yet be Rome amidst thine anguish,
Fight as thou wast wont to vanquish!

VIII.
Yet once more, ye old Penates!
Let not your quenched hearts be Atés!
Yet again, ye shadowy Heroes,
Yield not to these stranger Neros!
Though the son who slew his mother
Shed Rome's blood, he was your brother:
'Twas the Roman curbed the Roman;—
Brennus was a baffled foeman.
Yet again, ye saints and martyrs,
Rise! for yours are holier charters!
Mighty Gods of temples falling,
Yet in ruin still appalling!
Mightier Founders of those altars,
True and Christian,—strike the assaulters!
Tiber! Tiber! let thy torrent
Show even Nature 's self abhorrent.
Let each breathing heart dilated
Turn, as doth the lion baited!
Rome be crushed to one wide tomb,
But be still the Roman's Rome!

[BOURBON, ARNOLD, CÆSAR, and others, arrive at the foot of the wall. ARNOLD is about to plant his ladder.

BOURBON - Hold, Arnold! I am first.

ARNOLD - Not so, my Lord.

BOURBON - Hold, sir, I charge you! Follow! I am proud
Of such a follower, but will brook no leader.

[BOURBON plants his ladder, and begins to moust.

Now, boys! On! on!

[A shot strikes him, and BOURBON falls.

CÆSAR - And off!

ARNOLD - Eternal powers!
The host will be appalled,—but vengeance! vengeance!

BOURBON - 'Tis nothing—lend me your hand.

[BOURBON takes ARNOLD by the hand, and rises; but as he puts his foot on the step, falls again.

Arnold! I am sped.
Conceal my fall—all will go well—conceal it!
Fling my cloak o'er what will be dust anon;
Let not the soldiers see it.

ARNOLD - You must be
Removed; the aid of—

BOURBON - No, my gallant boy!
Death is upon me. But what is one life?
The Bourbon's spirit shall command them still.
Keep them yet ignorant that I am but clay,
Till they are conquerors—then do as you may.

CÆSAR - Would not your Highness choose to kiss the cross?
We have no priest here, but the hilt of sword
May serve instead:—it did the same for Bayard.

BOURBON - Thou bitter slave! to name him at this time!
But I deserve it.

ARNOLD - (to CÆSAR).
Villain, hold your peace!

CÆSAR - What, when a Christian dies? Shall I not offer
A Christian "Vade in pace?"

ARNOLD - Silence! Oh!
Those eyes are glazing which o'erlooked the world,
And saw no equal.

BOURBON - Arnold, shouldst thou see
France—But hark! hark! the assault grows warmer—Oh!
For but an hour, a minute more of life,
To die within the wall! Hence, Arnold, hence!
You lose time—they will conquer Rome without thee.

ARNOLD - And without thee.

BOURBON - Not so; I'll lead them still
In spirit. Cover up my dust, and breathe not
That I have ceased to breathe. Away! and be
Victorious.

ARNOLD - But I must not leave thee thus.

BOURBON - You must—farewell—Up! up! the world is winning.

[BOURBON dies.

CÆSAR - (to ARNOLD).
Come, Count, to business.

ARNOLD - True. I'll weep hereafter.

[ARNOLD covers BOURBON'S body with a mantle, mounts the ladder, crying

The Bourbon! Bourbon! On, boys! Rome is ours!

CÆSAR - Good night, Lord Constable! thou wert a Man.

[CÆSAR follows ARNOLD; they reach the battlement; ARNOLD and CÆSAR are struck down.

CÆSAR - A precious somerset! Is your countship injured?

ARNOLD - No.

[Remounts the ladder.

CÆSAR - A rare blood-hound, when his own is heated!
And 'tis no boy's play. Now he strikes them down!
His hand is on the battlement—he grasps it
As though it were an altar; now his foot
Is on it, and—What have we here?—a Roman?
The first bird of the covey! he has fallen

[A MAN falls.

On the outside of the nest. Why, how now, fellow?

WOUNDED MAN - A drop of water!

CÆSAR - Blood's the only liquid
Nearer than Tiber.

WOUNDED MAN - I have died for Rome.

[Dies.

CÆSAR - And so did Bourbon, in another sense.
Oh, these immortal men! and their great motives!
But I must after my young charge. He is
By this time i' the Forum. Charge! charge!

[CÆSAR mounts the ladder; the scene closes.

SCENE II

—The City.—Combats between the Besiegers and Besieged in the streets. Inhabitants flying in confusion.

Enter C ÆSAR.

CÆSAR - I cannot find my hero; he is mixed
With the heroic crowd that now pursue
The fugitives, or battle with the desperate.
What have we here? A Cardinal or two
That do not seem in love with martyrdom.
How the old red-shanks scamper! Could they doff
Their hose as they have doffed their hats, 'twould be
A blessing, as a mark the less for plunder.
But let them fly; the crimson kennels now
Will not much stain their stockings, since the mire
Is of the self-same purple hue.

Enter a Party fighting—ARNOLD at the head of the Besiegers.

He comes,
Hand in hand with the mild twins—Gore and Glory.
Holla! hold, Count!

ARNOLD - Away! they must not rally.

CÆSAR - I tell thee, be not rash; a golden bridge
Is for a flying enemy. I gave thee
A form of beauty, and an
Exemption from some maladies of body,
But not of mind, which is not mine to give.
But though I gave the form of Thetis' son,
I dipped thee not in Styx; and 'gainst a foe
I would not warrant thy chivalric heart
More than Pelides; heel; why, then, be cautious,
And know thyself a mortal still.

ARNOLD - And who
With aught of soul would combat if he were
Invulnerable? That were pretty sport.
Think'st thou I beat for hares when lions roar?

[ARNOLD rushes into the combat.

CÆSAR - A precious sample of humanity!
Well, his blood's up; and, if a little 's shed,
'Twill serve to curb his fever.

[ARNOLD engages with a ROMAN, who retires towards a portico.

ARNOLD - Yield thee, slave!
I promise quarter.

ROMAN - That's soon said.

ARNOLD - And done—
My word is known.

ROMAN - So shall be my deeds.
[They re-engage. Cæsar comes forward.

CÆSAR - Why, Arnold! hold thine own: thou hast in hand
A famous artisan, a cunning sculptor;
Also a dealer in the sword and dagger.
Not so, my musqueteer; 'twas he who slew
The Bourbon from the wall.

ARNOLD - Aye, did he so?
Then he hath carved his monument.

ROMAN - I yet
May live to carve your better's.

CÆSAR - Well said, my man of marble! Benvenuto,
Thou hast some practice in both ways; and he
Who slays Cellini will have worked as hard
As e'er thou didst upon Carrara's blocks.

[ARNOLD disarms and wounds CELLINI, but slightly: the latter draws a pistol, and fires; then retires, and disappears through the portico.

CÆSAR - How farest thou? Thou hast a taste, methinks,
Of red Bellona's banquet.

ARNOLD - (staggers).
'Tis a scratch.
Lend me thy scarf. He shall not 'scape me thus.

CÆSAR - Where is it?

ARNOLD - In the shoulder, not the sword arm—
And that 's enough. I am thirsty: would I had
A helm of water!

CÆSAR - That's a liquid now
In requisition, but by no means easiest
To come at.

ARNOLD - And my thirst increases;—but
I'll find a way to quench it.

CÆSAR - Or be quenched
Thyself.

ARNOLD - The chance is even; we will throw
The dice thereon. But I lose time in prating;
Prithee be quick.

[CÆSAR binds on the scarf.

And what dost thou so idly?
Why dost not strike?

CÆSAR - Your old philosophers
Beheld mankind, as mere spectators of
The Olympic games. When I behold a prize
Worth wrestling for, I may be found a Milo.

ARNOLD - Aye, 'gainst an oak.

CÆSAR - A forest, when it suits me:
I combat with a mass, or not at all.
Meantime, pursue thy sport as I do mine;
Which is just now to gaze, since all these labourers
Will reap my harvest gratis.

ARNOLD - Thou art still
A fiend!

CÆSAR - And thou—a man.

ARNOLD - Why, such I fain would show me.

CÆSAR - True—as men are.

ARNOLD - And what is that?

CÆSAR -
Thou feelest and thou see'st.

[Exit ARNOLD, joining in the combat which still continues between detached parties. The scene
closes.

SCENE III

—St. Peter's—The interior of the Church—The Pope at the Altar—Priests, etc., crowding in
confusion, and Citizens flying for refuge, pursued by Soldiery.

Enter CÆSAR.

A SPANISH SOLDIER - Down with them, comrades, seize upon those lamps!
Cleave yon bald-pated shaveling to the chine!
His rosary 's of gold!

LUTHERAN SOLDIER - Revenge! revenge!
Plunder hereafter, but for vengeance now—
Yonder stands Anti-Christ!

CÆSAR - (interposing).
How now, schismatic?
What wouldst thou?

LUTHERAN SOLDIER - In the holy name of Christ,
Destroy proud Anti-Christ. I am a Christian.

CÆSAR - Yea, a disciple that would make the founder
Of your belief renounce it, could he see
Such proselytes. Best stint thyself to plunder.

LUTHERAN SOLDIER - I say he is the Devil.

CÆSAR - Hush! keep that secret,
Lest he should recognise you for his own.

LUTHERAN SOLDIER - Why would you save him? I repeat he is
The Devil, or the Devil's vicar upon earth.

CÆSAR - And that's the reason: would you make a quarrel
With your best friends? You had far best be quiet;
His hour is not yet come.

LUTHERAN SOLDIER - That shall be seen!

[The LUTHERAN SOLDIER rushes forward: a shot strikes him from one of the Pope's Guards, and he falls at the foot of the Altar.

CÆSAR - (to the Lutheran).
I told you so.

LUTHERAN SOLDIER - And will you not avenge me?

CÆSAR - Not I! You know that "Vengeance is the Lord's:"
You see he loves no interlopers.

LUTHERAN SOLDIER - (dying).
Oh!
Had I but slain him, I had gone on high,
Crowned with eternal glory! Heaven, forgive
My feebleness of arm that reached him not,
And take thy servant to thy mercy. 'Tis
A glorious triumph still; proud Babylon 's
No more; the Harlot of the Seven Hills
Hath changed her scarlet raiment for sackcloth
And ashes!

[The LUTHERAN SOLDIER dies.

CÆSAR - Yes, thine own amidst the rest.
Well done, old Babel!

[The GUARDS defend themselves desperately, while the Pontiff escapes, by a private passage, to the Vatican and the Castle of St. Angelo.

CÆSAR - Ha! right nobly battled!
Now, priest! now, soldier! the two great professions,
Together by the ears and hearts! I have not
Seen a more comic pantomime since Titus
Took Jewry. But the Romans had the best then;
Now they must take their turn.

SOLDIERS - He hath escaped!
Follow!

ANOTHER SOLDIER - They have barred the narrow passage up,
And it is clogged with dead even to the door.

CÆSAR - I am glad he hath escaped: he may thank me for't
In part. I would not have his bulls abolished—
'Twere worth one half our empire: his indulgences
Demand some in return; no, no, he must not
Fall;—and besides, his now escape may furnish
A future miracle, in future proof
Of his infallibility.

[To the SPANISH SOLDIERY.

Well, cut-throats!
What do you pause for? If you make not haste,
There will not be a link of pious gold left.
And you, too, Catholics! Would ye return
From such a pilgrimage without a relic?
The very Lutherans have more true devotion:
See how they strip the shrines!

SOLDIERS - By holy Peter!
He speaks the truth; the heretics will bear
The best away.

CÆSAR - And that were shame! Go to!
Assist in their conversion.

[The SOLDIERS disperse; many quit the Church, others enter.

CÆSAR - They are gone,
And others come: so flows the wave on wave

Of what these creatures call Eternity,
Deeming themselves the breakers of the Ocean,
While they are but its bubbles, ignorant
That foam is their foundation. So, another!

Enter OLIMPIA, flying from the pursuit—She springs upon the Altar.

SOLDIER - She's mine!

ANOTHER SOLDIER - (opposing the former).
You lie, I tracked her first: and were she
The Pope's niece, I'll not yield her.

[They fight.

3RD SOLDIER - (advancing towards OLIMPIA).
You may settle
Your claims; I'll make mine good.

OLIMPIA -
Infernal slave!
You touch me not alive.

3RD SOLDIER - Alive or dead!

OLIMPIA - (embracing a massive crucifix).
Respect your God!

3RD SOLDIER - Yes, when he shines in gold.
Girl, you but grasp your dowry.

[As he advances, OLIMPIA, with a strong and sudden effort, casts down the crucifix; it strikes the
SOLDIER, who falls.

3RD SOLDIER - Oh, great God!

OLIMPIA - Ah! now you recognise him.

3RD SOLDIER - My brain 's crushed!
Comrades, help, ho! All's darkness!

[He dies.

OTHER SOLDIERS - (coming up).
Slay her, although she had a thousand lives:
She hath killed our comrade.

OLIMPIA - Welcome such a death!
You have no life to give, which the worst slave
Would take. Great God! through thy redeeming Son,
And thy Son's Mother, now receive me as

I would approach thee, worthy her, and him, and thee!

Enter ARNOLD.

ARNOLD - What do I see? Accurséd jackals!
Forbear!

CÆSAR - (aside and laughing).
Ha! ha! here 's equity! The dogs
Have as much right as he. But to the issue!

SOLDIERS - Count, she hath slain our comrade.

ARNOLD - With what weapon?

SOLDIERS - The cross, beneath which he is crushed; behold him
Lie there, more like a worm than man; she cast it
Upon his head.

ARNOLD - Even so: there is a woman
Worthy a brave man's liking. Were ye such,
Ye would have honoured her. But get ye hence,
And thank your meanness, other God you have none,
For your existence. Had you touched a hair
Of those dishevelled locks, I would have thinned
Your ranks more than the enemy. Away!
Ye jackals! gnaw the bones the lion leaves,
But not even these till he permits.

A SOLDIER - (murmuring).
The lion
Might conquer for himself then.

ARNOLD - (cuts him down).
Mutineer!
Rebel in hell—you shall obey on earth!

[The SOLDIERS assault ARNOLD.

ARNOLD - Come on! I'm glad on't! I will show you, slaves,

How you should be commanded, and who led you
First o'er the wall you were so shy to scale,
Until I waved my banners from its height,
As you are bold within it.

[ARNOLD mows down the foremost; the rest throw down their arms.

SOLDIERS - Mercy! mercy!

ARNOLD - Then learn to grant it. Have I taught you who

Led you o'er Rome's eternal battlements?

SOLDIERS - We saw it, and we know it; yet forgive
A moment's error in the heat of conquest—
The conquest which you led to.

ARNOLD - Get you hence!
Hence to your quarters! you will find them fixed
In the Colonna palace.

OLIMPIA - (aside).
In my father's
House!

ARNOLD - (to the Soldiers).
Leave your arms; ye have no further need
Of such: the city 's rendered. And mark well
You keep your hands clean, or I'll find out a stream
As red as Tiber now runs, for your baptism.

SOLDIERS - (deposing their arms and departing).
We obey!

ARNOLD - (to Olimpia).
Lady, you are safe.

OLIMPIA - I should be so,
Had I a knife even; but it matters not—
Death hath a thousand gates; and on the marble,
Even at the altar foot, whence I look down
Upon destruction, shall my head be dashed,
Ere thou ascend it. God forgive thee, man!

ARNOLD - I wish to merit his forgiveness, and
Thine own, although I have not injured thee.

OLIMPIA - No! Thou hast only sacked my native land,—
No injury!—and made my father's house
A den of thieves! No injury!—this temple—
Slippery with Roman and with holy gore!
No injury! And now thou wouldst preserve me,
To be—but that shall never be!

[She raises her eyes to Heaven, folds her robe round her, and prepares to dash herself down on the side of the Altar opposite to that where ARNOLD stands.

ARNOLD - Hold! hold!
I swear.

OLIMPIA - Spare thine already forfeit soul
A perjury for which even Hell would loathe thee.

I know thee.

ARNOLD - No, thou know'st me not; I am not
Of these men, though—

OLIMPIA - I judge thee by thy mates;
It is for God to judge thee as thou art.
I see thee purple with the blood of Rome;
Take mine, 'tis all thou e'er shalt have of me,
And here, upon the marble of this temple,
Where the baptismal font baptized me God's,
I offer him a blood less holy
But not less pure (pure as it left me then,
A redeeméd infant) than the holy water
The saints have sanctified!

[OLIMPIA waves her hand to ARNOLD with disdain, and dashes herself on the pavement from the Altar.

ARNOLD - Eternal God!
I feel thee now! Help! help! she's gone.

CÆSAR - (approaches).
I am here.

ARNOLD - Thou! but oh, save her!

CÆSAR - (assisting him to raise OLIMPIA).
She hath done it well!
The leap was serious.

ARNOLD - Oh! she is lifeless!

CÆSAR - If
She be so, I have nought to do with that:
The resurrection is beyond me.

ARNOLD - Slave!

CÆSAR - Aye, slave or master, 'tis all one: methinks
Good words, however, are as well at times.

ARNOLD - Words!—Canst thou aid her?

CÆSAR - I will try. A sprinkling
Of that same holy water may be useful.

[He brings some in his helmet from the font.

ARNOLD - 'Tis mixed with blood.

CÆSAR - There is no cleaner now
In Rome.

ARNOLD - How pale! how beautiful! how lifeless!
Alive or dead, thou Essence of all Beauty,
I love but thee!

CÆSAR - Even so Achilles loved
Penthesilea; with his form it seems
You have his heart, and yet it was no soft one.

ARNOLD - She breathes! But no, 'twas nothing, or the last
Faint flutter Life disputes with Death.

CÆSAR - She breathes.

ARNOLD - Thou say'st it? Then 'tis truth.

CÆSAR - You do me right—
The Devil speaks truth much oftener than he's deemed:
He hath an ignorant audience.

ARNOLD - (without attending to him).
Yes! her heart beats.
Alas! that the first beat of the only heart
I ever wished to beat with mine should vibrate
To an assassin's pulse.

CÆSAR - A sage reflection,
But somewhat late i' the day. Where shall we bear her?
I say she lives.

ARNOLD - And will she live?

CÆSAR - As much
As dust can.

ARNOLD - Then she is dead!

CÆSAR - Bah! bah! You are so,
And do not know it. She will come to life—
Such as you think so, such as you now are;
But we must work by human means.

ARNOLD - We will
Convey her unto the Colonna palace,
Where I have pitched my banner.

CÆSAR - Come then! raise her up!

ARNOLD - Softly!

CÆSAR - As softly as they bear the dead,
Perhaps because they cannot feel the jolting.

ARNOLD - But doth she live indeed?

CÆSAR - Nay, never fear!
But, if you rue it after, blame not me.

ARNOLD - Let her but live!

CÆSAR - The Spirit of her life
Is yet within her breast, and may revive.
Count! count! I am your servant in all things,
And this is a new office:—'tis not oft
I am employed in such; but you perceive
How staunch a friend is what you call a fiend.
On earth you have often only fiends for friends;
Now I desert not mine. Soft! bear her hence,
The beautiful half-clay, and nearly spirit!
I am almost enamoured of her, as
Of old the Angels of her earliest sex.

ARNOLD - Thou!

CÆSAR - I! But fear not. I'll not be your rival.

ARNOLD - Rival!

CÆSAR - I could be one right formidable;
But since I slew the seven husbands of
Tobias' future bride (and after all
Was smoked out by some incense), I have laid
Aside intrigue: 'tis rarely worth the trouble
Of gaining, or—what is more difficult—
Getting rid of your prize again; for there's
The rub! at least to mortals.

ARNOLD - Prithee, peace!
Softly! methinks her lips move, her eyes open!

CÆSAR - Like stars, no doubt; for that 's a metaphor
For Lucifer and Venus.

ARNOLD - To the palace
Colonna, as I told you!

CÆSAR - Oh! I know
My way through Rome.

ARNOLD - Now onward, onward! Gently!

[Exeunt, bearing OLIMPIA. The scene closes.

PART III

SCENE I

—A Castle in the Apennines, surrounded by a wild but smiling Country. CHORUS of Peasants singing before the Gates.

CHORUS
I.
The wars are over,
The spring is come;
The bride and her lover
Have sought their home:
They are happy, we rejoice;
Let their hearts have an echo in every voice!

II.
The spring is come; the violet 's gone,
The first-born child of the early sun:
With us she is but a winter's flower,
The snow on the hills cannot blast her bower,
And she lifts up her dewy eye of blue
To the youngest sky of the self-same hue.

III.
And when the spring comes with her host
Of flowers, that flower beloved the most
Shrinks from the crowd that may confuse
Her heavenly odour and virgin hues.

IV.
Pluck the others, but still remember
Their herald out of dim December—
The morning star of all the flowers,
The pledge of daylight's lengthened hours;
Nor, midst the roses, e'er forget
The virgin—virgin Violet.

Enter C ÆSAR .

CÆSAR - (singing).
The wars are all over,
Our swords are all idle,
The steed bites the bridle,
The casque 's on the wall.
There 's rest for the rover;

But his armour is rusty,
And the veteran grows crusty,
As he yawns in the hall.
He drinks—but what 's drinking?
A mere pause from thinking!
No bugle awakes him with life-and-death call.

CHORUS - But the hound bayeth loudly,
The boar 's in the wood,
And the falcon longs proudly
To spring from her hood:
On the wrist of the noble
She sits like a crest,
And the air is in trouble
With birds from their nest.

CÆSAR - Oh! shadow of Glory!
Dim image of War!
But the chase hath no story,
Her hero no star,
Since Nimrod, the founder
Of empire and chase,
Who made the woods wonder
And quake for their race.
When the lion was young,
In the pride of his might,
Then 'twas sport for the strong
To embrace him in fight;
To go forth, with a pine
For a spear, 'gainst the mammoth,
Or strike through the ravine
At the foaming behemoth;

While man was in stature
As towers in our time,
The first born of Nature,
And, like her, sublime!

CHORUS - But the wars are over,
The spring is come;
The bride and her lover
Have sought their home:
They are happy, and we rejoice;
Let their hearts have an echo from every voice!

[Exeunt the PEASANTRY, singing.

FRAGMENT OF THE THIRD PART

CHORUS - When the merry bells are ringing,
And the peasant girls are singing,
And the early flowers are flinging
Their odours in the air;
And the honey bee is clinging
To the buds; and birds are winging
Their way, pair by pair:
Then the earth looks free from trouble
With the brightness of a bubble:
Though I did not make it,
I could breathe on and break it;
But too much I scorn it,
Or else I would mourn it,
To see despots and slaves
Playing o'er their own graves.

Enter Count ARNOLD.

ARNOLD - You are merry, Sir—what? singing too?

C ÆSAR - It is
The land of Song—and Canticles you know
Were once my avocation.

ARNOLD - Nothing moves you;
You scoff even at your own calamity—

And such calamity! how wert thou fallen
Son of the Morning! and yet Lucifer
Can smile.

CÆSAR - His shape can—would you have me weep,
In the fair form I wear, to please you?

ARNOLD - Ah!

CÆSAR - You are grave—what have you on your spirit!

ARNOLD - Nothing.

CÆSAR - How mortals lie by instinct! If you ask
A disappointed courtier—What's the matter?
"Nothing"—an outshone Beauty what has made
Her smooth brow crisp—"Oh, Nothing!"—a young heir
When his Sire has recovered from the Gout,
What ails him? "Nothing!" or a Monarch who
Has heard the truth, and looks imperial on it—
What clouds his royal aspect? "Nothing," "Nothing!"
Nothing—eternal nothing—of these nothings
All are a lie—for all to them are much!
And they themselves alone the real "Nothings."

Your present Nothing, too, is something to you—
What is it?

ARNOLD - Know you not?

CÆSAR - I only know
What I desire to know! and will not waste
Omniscience upon phantoms. Out with it!
If you seek aid from me—or else be silent.
And eat your thoughts—till they breed snakes within you.

ARNOLD - Olimpia!

CÆSAR - I thought as much—go on.

ARNOLD - I thought she had loved me.

CÆSAR - Blessings on your Creed!
What a good Christian you were found to be!
But what cold Sceptic hath appalled your faith
And transubstantiated to crumbs again
The body of your Credence?

ARNOLD - No one—but—
Each day—each hour—each minute shows me more
And more she loves me not—

CÆSAR - Doth she rebel?

ARNOLD - No, she is calm, and meek, and silent with me,
And coldly dutiful, and proudly patient—
Endures my Love—not meets it.

CÆSAR - That seems strange.
You are beautiful and brave! the first is much
For passion—and the rest for Vanity.

ARNOLD - I saved her life, too; and her Father's life,
And Father's house from ashes.

CÆSAR - These are nothing.
You seek for Gratitude—the Philosopher's stone.

ARNOLD - And find it not.

CÆSAR - You cannot find what is not.
But found would it content you? would you owe
To thankfulness what you desire from Passion?
No! No! you would be loved—what you call loved—
Self-loved—loved for yourself—for neither health,
Nor wealth, nor youth, nor power, nor rank, nor beauty—

For these you may be stript of—but beloved
As an abstraction—for—you know not what!
These are the wishes of a moderate lover—
And so you love.

ARNOLD - Ah! could I be beloved,
Would I ask wherefore?

CÆSAR - Yes! and not believe
The answer—You are jealous.

ARNOLD - And of whom?

CÆSAR - It may be of yourself, for Jealousy
Is as a shadow of the Sun. The Orb
Is mighty—as you mortals deem—and to
Your little Universe seems universal;
But, great as He appears, and is to you,
The smallest cloud—the slightest vapour of
Your humid earth enables you to look
Upon a Sky which you revile as dull;
Though your eyes dare not gaze on it when cloudless.
Nothing can blind a mortal like to light.
Now Love in you is as the Sun—a thing
Beyond you—and your Jealousy 's of Earth—
A cloud of your own raising.

ARNOLD - Not so always!
There is a cause at times.

CÆSAR - Oh, yes! when atoms jostle,
The System is in peril. But I speak
Of things you know not. Well, to earth again!
This precious thing of dust—this bright Olimpia—
This marvellous Virgin, is a marble maid—
An Idol, but a cold one to your heat
Promethean, and unkindled by your torch.

ARNOLD - Slave!

CÆSAR - In the victor's Chariot, when Rome triumphed,
There was a Slave of yore to tell him truth!
You are a Conqueror—command your Slave.

ARNOLD - Teach me the way to win the woman's love.

CÆSAR - Leave her.

ARNOLD - Where that the path—I'd not pursue it.

CÆSAR - No doubt! for if you did, the remedy

Would be for a disease already cured.

ARNOLD - All wretched as I am, I would not quit
My unrequited love, for all that 's happy.

CÆSAR - You have possessed the woman—still possess.
What need you more?

ARNOLD - To be myself possessed—
To be her heart as she is mine.

Lord Byron – A Short Biography

Byron, one of England's greatest poets, endured a quite difficult background. His father, Captain John "Mad Jack" Byron had married his second wife, the former Catherine Gordon, a descendant of Cardinal Beaton and heiress of the Gight estate in Aberdeenshire, Scotland for the same reason that he married his first: her money. Byron's mother-to-be had to sell her land and title to pay her new husband's debts and within two years the large estate of £23,500, had been squandered, leaving her with an annual income in trust of £150. In a move to avoid his creditors, Catherine accompanied her husband to France in 1786, but returned to England at the end of 1787 in order to give birth to her son on English soil.

George Gordon Byron was born on January 22nd 1788, in lodgings, at Holles Street in London although there is a conflicting account of him having been born in Dover.

He was christened, at St Marylebone Parish Church, George Gordon Byron, after his maternal grandfather, George Gordon of Gight, a descendant of James I of Scotland, who, in 1779, had committed suicide.

In 1790 Catherine moved back to Aberdeenshire and it was here that Byron spent his childhood. His father joined them in their lodgings in Queen Street, but the couple quickly separated. Catherine was prone to mood swings and melancholy. Her husband continued to borrow money from her and she fell deeper into debt. It was one of these "loans" that allowed him to travel to Valenciennes, France, where he died in 1791.

When Byron's great-uncle, the "wicked" Lord Byron, died on 21 May 1798, the 10-year-old boy became the 6th Baron Byron of Rochdale and inherited the ancestral home, Newstead Abbey, in Nottinghamshire. However the Abbey was in a state of disrepair and it was leased to Lord Grey de Ruthyn, and others for several years.

Catherine's parenting swung between either spoiling or indulging her son to stubbornly refusing every plea. Her drinking disgusted him, and he mocked her short and corpulent frame. She did retaliate and, in a fit of temper, once called him as "a lame brat", on account of his club-foot, an issue on which we was very sensitive. He referred to himself as "le diable boiteux" ("the limping devil").

Byron early education was taken at Aberdeen Grammar School, and in August 1799 he entered the school of Dr. William Glennie, in Dulwich. He was encouraged to exercise in moderation but could not restrain himself from "violent" bouts in an attempt to overcompensate for his deformed foot.

His mother interfered, often withdrawing him from school, and resulting in him lacking discipline and neglecting his classical studies.

In 1801 he was sent to Harrow, where he remained until July 1805. Byron was an excellent orator but undistinguished student and an unskilled cricketer but strangely he did represent the school in the very first Eton v Harrow cricket match at Lord's in 1805.

Byron, always prone to over-indulge, fell in love with Mary Chaworth, whom he met while at school, and thence refused to return to Harrow in September 1803. His mother wrote, "He has no indisposition that I know of but love, desperate love, the worst of all maladies in my opinion. In short, the boy is distractedly in love with Miss Chaworth."

He did finally return in January 1804, and described his friends there; "My school friendships were with me passions for I was always violent." His nostalgic poems about his Harrow friendships, in his book Childish Recollections, published in 1806, talk of a "consciousness of sexual differences that may in the end make England untenable to him".

The following autumn he attended Trinity College, Cambridge, where he met and formed a close bond with John Edleston. On his "protégé" Byron wrote, "He has been my almost constant associate since October, 1805, when I entered Trinity College. His voice first attracted my attention, his countenance fixed it, and his manners attached me to him forever." In his memory Byron composed Thyrza, a series of elegies. In later years Byron described the affair as "a violent, though pure love and passion". The public were beginning to view homosexuality with increasing distaste and the law now specified such sanctions as public hanging against convicted or even suspected offenders. Though equally Byron may just be using 'pure' out of respect for Edleston's innocence, in contrast to the more sexually overt relations experienced at Harrow School. Byron is now thought of as bi-sexual though more fulfilled, on all levels, by women.

While not at school or college, Byron lived with his mother in Southwell, Nottinghamshire. While there, he cultivated friendships with Elizabeth Pigot and her brother, John, with whom he staged two plays for the entertainment of the local community. During this time, with the help of Elizabeth, who copied his rough drafts, he wrote his first volumes of poetry, Fugitive Pieces, which included poems written when Byron was only 14. However, it was promptly recalled and burned on the advice of his friend, the Reverend J. T. Becher, on account of its more amorous verses, particularly the poem To Mary.

Hours of Idleness, which collected many of the previous poems, along with recent compositions, was the culminating book. The savage, anonymous criticism this received in the Edinburgh Review prompted his first major satire, English Bards and Scotch Reviewers in 1809. This was put into the hands of his relative, R. C. Dallas, requesting him to "...get it published without his name". Although published anonymously Byron was generally known to be the author. The work so upset some of his critics they challenged Byron to a duel. Of course, over time, it became a mark of renown to be the target of Byron's pen.

Byron first took his seat in the House of Lords March 13th, 1809. He was a strong advocate of social reform, and one of the few Parliamentary defenders of the Luddites: specifically, he was against a death penalty for Luddite "frame breakers" in Nottinghamshire, who destroyed the textile machines that were putting them out of work. His first speech before the Lords, on February 27th, 1812, sarcastically referenced the "benefits" of automation, which he saw as producing inferior material as well as putting people out of work, and concluded the proposed law was only missing two things to be effective: "Twelve Butchers for a Jury and a Jeffries for a Judge!"

Two months later, Byron made another impassioned speech before the House in support of Catholic emancipation. He expressed opposition to the established religion because it was unfair to people who practiced other faiths.

Out of this period would follow several overtly political poems; Song for the Luddites (1816), The Landlords' Interest, Canto XIV of The Age of Bronze, Wellington: The Best of the Cut-Throats (1819) and The Intellectual Eunuch Castlereagh (1818).

Like his father Byron racked up numerous debts. His mother thought he had "reckless disregard for money" and lived in fear of her son's creditors.

Between1809 to 1811, Byron went on the Grand Tour, then customary for a young nobleman. The Napoleonic Wars meant most of Europe had to be avoided, and he instead ventured south to the Mediterranean.

There is some correspondence among his circle of Cambridge friends that suggests that another motive was the hope of homosexual experience, and other theories saying that he was worried about a possible dalliance with a married woman, Mary Chaworth, his former love.

But other possibilities exist. Byron had read much about the Ottoman and Persian lands as a child, was attracted to Islam (especially Sufi mysticism), and later wrote, "With these countries, and events connected with them, all my really poetical feelings begin and end."

Byron began his trip in Portugal from where he wrote a letter to his friend Mr. Hodgson in which he describes his mastery of the Portuguese language, consisting mainly of swearing and insults. Byron particularly enjoyed his stay in Sintra that is described in Childe Harold's Pilgrimage as "glorious Eden". From Lisbon he travelled overland to Seville, Jerez de la Frontera, Cádiz, Gibraltar and from there by sea on to Malta and Greece.

While in Athens, Byron met 14-year-old Nicolò Giraud, who became quite close and taught him Italian. Byron sent Giraud to school at a monastery in Malta and in his will, though later taken out, bequeathed him a sizeable sum.

Byron then moved on to Smyrna, and then Constantinople on board HMS Salsette. While HMS Salsette was anchored awaiting Ottoman permission to dock at the city, on May 3rd, 1810 Byron and Lieutenant Ekenhead, of Salsette 's Marines, swam the Hellespont. Byron commemorated this feat in the second canto of Don Juan.

When he sailed back to England in April 1811, he travelled, for a time, aboard the transport ship Hydra, which had on board the last large shipments of Lord Elgin's marbles, a piece of vandalism that Byron had longed railed against. The last leg of his voyage home was from Malta in aboard HMS Volage. He arrived at Sheerness, Kent, on July 14th. He was home after two years away.

On August 2nd, his mother died. "I had but one friend in the world," he exclaimed, "and she is gone."

The following year, 1812, Byron became a sensation with the publication, via his literary agent and family relative R. C. Dallas, of the first two cantos of 'Childe Harold's Pilgrimage'. He rapidly became the most brilliant star in the dazzling world of Regency London, sought after at every society venue, elected to several exclusive clubs, and frequented the most fashionable London drawing-rooms. His own words recall; "I awoke one morning and found myself famous". The Edinburgh Review allowed that Byron had "improved marvellously since his last appearance at our tribunal." He followed up his success with the poem's last two cantos, as well as four equally celebrated "Oriental Tales": The Giaour, The Bride of Abydos, The Corsair and Lara.

His affair with Lady Caroline Lamb (who called him "mad, bad and dangerous to know"), as well as other women and the constant pressure of debt, caused him to seek a suitable marriage i.e. marry wealth. One choice was Annabella Milbanke. But in 1813 he met again, after four years, his half-sister, Augusta Leigh. Rumours of incest constantly surrounded the pair; Augusta, who was married, gave birth on April 15th, 1814 to her third daughter, Elizabeth Medora Leigh, and Byron is suspected to be the father.

To escape from debts and rumours he now sought, in earnest, to marry Annabella, (said to be the likely heiress of a rich uncle). They married on January 2nd, 1815, and their daughter, Ada, was born in December of that year. However Byron's continuing obsession with Augusta and dalliances with others made their marriage a misery.

Annabella thought Byron insane and she left him, taking Ada, in January 1816 and began proceedings for a legal separation. For Byron the scandal of the separation, the continuing rumours about Augusta, and ever-increasing debts were to now force him to leave England.

He passed through Belgium and along the river Rhine and by the summer was settled at the Villa Diodati by Lake Geneva, Switzerland, with his personal physician, the young, brilliant, and handsome John William Polidori. There Byron befriended the poet Percy Bysshe Shelley, and his future wife Mary Godwin. He was also joined by Mary's stepsister, Claire Clairmont, with whom, almost inevitably, he had had an affair with in London.

Kept indoors at the Villa Diodati by the incessant rain during three days in June, the five turned to writing. Mary Shelley produced what would become Frankenstein, or The Modern Prometheus, and Polidori was inspired by a fragmentary story of Byron's, Fragment of a Novel, to produce The Vampyre, the progenitor of the romantic vampire genre.

Byron's story fragment was published as a postscript to Mazeppa; he also now wrote the third canto of Childe Harold.

Byron wintered in Venice, pausing his travels when he fell in love with Marianna Segati, in whose Venice house he was lodging, but who was soon replaced by 22-year-old Margarita Cogni; both women were married. Cogni, who could not read or write, left her husband to move into Byron's Venice house. Their fighting often caused Byron to spend nights in his gondola; when he asked her to leave the house, she threw herself into the Venetian canal.

In a visit to San Lazzaro degli Armeni in Venice, he began to immerse himself in Armenian culture. He learned the Armenian language, and attended many seminars about language and history. He co-authored English Grammar and Armenian in 1817, and Armenian Grammar and English in 1819, where he included quotations from classical and modern Armenian and later, in 1821, participated in the compilation of the English Armenian dictionary, and in the preface he mapped out the relationship of the Armenians with, and the oppression of, the Turkish "pashas" and the Persian satraps, and their struggle for liberation.

In 1817 after a visit to Rome and back in Venice, he wrote the fourth canto of Childe Harold and sold his ancestral home, Newstead Abbey, as well as publishing Manfred; A Dramatic Poem and , Cain; A Mystery.

Byron wrote the first five cantos of his renowned Don Juan between 1818 and 1820. And besides work and adventure there was always love. Women, of course, were always in evidence and the young Countess Teresa Guiccioli found her first love in Byron, who in turn asked her to elope with him. They lived in Ravenna between 1819 and 1821 where he continued Don Juan and also wrote the Ravenna Diary, My Dictionary and Recollections.

It was here that he now received visits from Percy Bysshe Shelley and Thomas Moore.

Of Byron's lifestyle in Ravenna Shelley informs us that; "Lord Byron gets up at two. I get up, quite contrary to my usual custom … at 12. After breakfast we sit talking till six. From six to eight we gallop through the pine forest which divide Ravenna from the sea; we then come home and dine, and sit up gossiping till six in the morning. I don't suppose this will kill me in a week or fortnight, but I shall not try it longer. Lord B.'s establishment consists, besides servants, of ten horses, eight enormous dogs, three monkeys, five cats, an eagle, a crow, and a falcon; and all these, except the horses, walk about the house, which every now and then resounds with their unarbitrated quarrels, as if they were the masters of it… . [P.S.] I find that my enumeration of the animals in this Circean Palace was defective …. I have just met on the grand staircase five peacocks, two guinea hens, and an Egyptian crane. I wonder who all these animals were before they were changed into these shapes."

From 1821 to 1822, he finished Cantos 6–12 of Don Juan at Pisa, and in the same year he joined with Leigh Hunt and Percy Bysshe Shelley in starting a short-lived newspaper, The Liberal, in the first number of which appeared The Vision of Judgment.

For the first time since his arrival in Italy, Byron found himself tempted to give dinner parties; his guests included the Shelleys, Edward Ellerker Williams, Thomas Medwin, John Taaffe and Edward John Trelawney; and "never", as Shelley said, "did he display himself to more advantage than on these occasions; being at once polite and cordial, full of social hilarity and the most perfect good humour; never diverging into ungraceful merriment, and yet keeping up the spirit of liveliness throughout the evening."

Byron's mother-in-law Judith Noel, the Hon. Lady Milbanke, died in 1822. Her will required that he change his surname to "Noel" in order for him to inherit half of her estate. He obtained a Royal Warrant allowing him to "take and use the surname of Noel only". The Royal Warrant also allowed him to "subscribe the said surname of Noel before all titles of honour", and from that point he signed himself "Noel Byron" (the usual signature of a peer being merely the peerage, in this case simply "Byron").

The Shelley's and Williams had rented a house on the coast and had a schooner built. Byron decided that he too should have his own yacht, and engaged Trelawny's friend, Captain Daniel Roberts, to design and construct the boat. It was named the Bolivar.

On July 8th, 1822 Shelley drowned in a boating accident. Byron attended the funeral. Shelley was cremated on the beach at Viareggio where his body had washed up. His ashes were later interred in Rome in the cemetery in Rome where lay already his son William and John Keats.

Byron was living in Genoa when, in 1823, while growing bored, he accepted a call for his help from representatives of the movement for Greek independence from the Ottoman Empire. With the assistance of his banker and Captain Daniel Roberts, Byron chartered the Brig Hercules to take him to Greece. On 16 July, Byron left Genoa arriving at Kefalonia in the Ionian Islands on August 4th.

Byron had spent £4,000 of his own money to refit the Greek fleet and sailed for Missolonghi in western Greece, arriving on December 29th, to join Alexandros Mavrokordatos, a Greek politician with military power. When the famous Danish sculptor Bertel Thorvaldsen heard about Byron's heroics in Greece, he voluntarily re-sculpted his earlier bust of Byron in Greek marble.

Mavrokordatos and Byron planned to attack the Turkish-held fortress of Lepanto, at the mouth of the Gulf of Corinth. Byron employed a fire-master to prepare artillery and took part of the rebel army under his own command, despite his lack of military experience. Before the expedition could sail, on February 15th, 1824, he fell ill, and the usual remedy of bloodletting weakened him further. He made a partial recovery, but in early April he caught a violent cold which further therapeutic bleeding, insisted on by his doctors, aggravated. He developed a violent fever, and died in Missolonghi on April 19th.

Alfred, Lord Tennyson would later recall the shocked reaction in Britain when word was received of Byron's death. The Greeks mourned Lord Byron deeply, and he became a hero. The Greek form of "Byron", continues in popularity as a name in Greece, and a town near Athens is called Vyronas in his honour.

Byron's body was embalmed, but the Greeks wanted their hero to stay with them. Some say his heart was removed to remain in Missolonghi. His body was returned to England (despite his dying wishes that it should not) for burial in Westminster Abbey, but the Abbey refused to accept it on the grounds of "questionable morality".

Huge crowds viewed his body as he lay in state for two days in London before being buried at the Church of St. Mary Magdalene in Hucknall, Nottinghamshire. A marble slab given by the King of Greece is laid directly above Byron's grave.

Byron's friends had raised the sum of £1,000 to commission a statue of the writer by the sculptor Thorvaldsen. However for a decade after the statue was completed, in 1834, most British institutions had refused to accept it, among them the British Museum, St. Paul's Cathedral, Westminster Abbey and the National Gallery, and it remained in storage. Finally Trinity College, Cambridge, placed the statue in its library.

Finally, in 1969, a145 years after Byron's death, a memorial to him was placed in Westminster Abbey. It had been pointedly noted by the New York Times that "People are beginning to ask whether this ignoring of Byron is not a thing of which England should be ashamed ... a bust or a tablet might be put in the Poets' Corner and England be relieved of ingratitude toward one of her really great sons." At last Byron was where he should be.

Lord Byron – A Concise Bibliography

The Major Works
Hours of Idleness (1807)
English Bards and Scotch Reviewers (1809)
Childe Harold's Pilgrimage, Cantos I & II (1812)
The Giaour (1813)

The Bride of Abydos (1813)
The Corsair (1814)
Lara, A Tale (1814)
Hebrew Melodies (1815)
The Siege of Corinth (1816)
Parisina (1816)
The Prisoner of Chillon (1816)
The Dream (1816)
Prometheus (1816)
Darkness (1816)
Manfred (1817)
The Lament of Tasso (1817)
Beppo (1818)
Childe Harold's Pilgrimage (1818)
Don Juan (1819–1824; incomplete on Byron's death in 1824)
Mazeppa (1819)
The Prophecy of Dante (1819)
Marino Faliero (1820)
Sardanapalus (1821)
The Two Foscari (1821)
Cain (1821)
The Vision of Judgment (1821)
Heaven and Earth (1821)
Werner (1822)
The Age of Bronze (1823)
The Island (1823)
The Deformed Transformed (1824)

Index of Titles (This is an abbreviated, not a complete, list of his poems).
A
Address, spoken at the Opening of Drury-Lane Theatre, Saturday, October 10, 1812
The Adieu
Adieu to the Muse (same as "Farewell to the Muse")
Address intended to be recited at the Caledonian Meeting
Adrian's Address to his Soul when Dying
The Age of Bronze (a transcription project)
"All is Vanity, Saith the Preacher"
And Thou Art Dead, as Young and Fair
And Wilt Thou Weep When I am Low?
Another Simple Ballat
Answer to —'s Professions of Affection
Answer to a Beautiful Poem
Answer to Some Elegant Verses Sent by a Friend to the Author, & etc.
Answer to the Foregoing, Addressed to Miss —
Aristomenes
Away, Away, Ye Notes of Woe!

B
Ballad

Beppo, a Venetian Story
The Blues, a Literary Eclogue
Bowles and Campbell
The Bride of Abydos, a Turkish Tale (A transcription project)
Bright Be the Place of Thy Soul! (see "Stanzas for Music")
By the Rivers of Babylon We Sat Down and Wept
"By the Waters of Babylon"

C

Cain, a Mystery (A transcription project)
The Chain I gave (same as "From the Turkish")
The Charity Ball
Childe Harold's Good Night (from Childe Harold's Pilgrimage, Canto I.)
Childe Harold's Pilgrimage
Childish Recollections
Churchill's Grave
The Conquest
The Cornelian
The Corsair: A Tale
The Curse of Minerva

D

Damætas
Darkness
The Death of Calmar and Orla
The Deformed Transformed, a drama (A transcription project)
The Destruction of Sennacherib
The Devil's Drive
Don Juan
A Dream (same as "Darkness")
The Dream
The Duel

E

E Nihilo Nihil; or, An Epigram Bewitched
Egotism. A Letter to J. T. Becher
Elegiac Stanzas on the Death of Sir Peter Parker, Bart.
Elegy
Elegy on Newstead Abbey
Elegy on the Death of Sir Peter Parker (same "Elegiac Stanzas on the Death of Sir Peter Parker, Bart.")
Endorsement to the Deed of Separation, in the April of 1816
English Bards, and Scotch Reviewers, a Satire
Epigram (If for Silver, or for Gold)
Epigram (In Digging up your Bones, Tom Paine)
Epigram (It Seems That the Braziers Propose Soon to Pass)
Epigram (The world is a bundle of hay)
Epigram on an Old Lady Who Had Some Curious Notions Respecting the Soul
Epigrams (Oh, Castlereagh! Thou Art a Patriot Now)
Epilogue
The Episode of Nisus and Euryalus (A Paraphrase from the Æneid, Lib. 9.)
Epistle from Mr. Murray to Dr. Polidori

Epistle to a Friend
Epistle to Augusta
Epistle to Mr. Murray
Epitaph
Epitaph for Joseph Blacket, Late Poet and Shoemaker
Epitaph for William Pitt
Epitaph on a Beloved Friend
Epitaph on a Friend (same as "Epitaph on a Beloved Friend")
Epitaph on John Adams, of Southwell
Epitaph to a Dog
Euthanasia

F
Fame, Wisdom, Love, and Power Were Mine (same as "All is Vanity, saith the Preacher")
Fare Thee Well
Farewell (same as "Farewell! if Ever Fondest Prayer")
Farewell Petition to J. C. H., Esqre.
Farewell to Malta
Farewell to the Muse
Fill the Goblet Again
The First Kiss of Love
A Fragment (Could I Remount the River of My Years)
Fragment (Hills of Annesley, Bleak and Barren)
A Fragment (When, to Their Airy Hall, my Fathers' Voice)
Fragment from the "Monk of Athos"
Fragment of a Translation from the 9th Book of Virgil's Æneid (compare "The Episode of Nisus and Euryalus")
Fragment of an Epistle to Thomas Moore
Fragments of School Exercises: From the "Prometheus Vinctus" of Æschylus
Francesca of Rimini
Francisca
From Anacreon Ode 3. ('Twas Now the Hour When Night Had Driven)
From Job (same as "A Spirit Passed Before Me")
From the French (Ægle, Beauty and Poet, Has Two Little Crimes)
From the French (Must Thou Go, my Glorious Chief)
From the Last Hill That Looks on Thy Once Holy Dome (same as "On the Day of the Destruction of Jerusalem by Titus")
From the Portuguese
From the Turkish (same as "The Chain I Gave")

G
G. G. B. to E. P. (same as "To M. S. G.") (When I Dream That You Love Me, you'll surely Forgive)
The Giaour
The Girl of Cadiz
Granta. A Medley

H
The Harp the Monarch Minstrel Swept
Heaven and Earth, a Mystery (A transcription project)
Hebrew Melodies
Herod's Lament for Mariamne

Love and Gold
A Love Song. To — (same as "Remind me not, Remind me not")
Love's Last Adieu
Lucietta. A Fragment

M

Maid of Athens, Ere We Part
Manfred, a Dramatic Poem
Marino Faliero, Doge of Venice, an Historical Tragedy (1821) (A transcription project)
Martial, Lib. I. Epig. I.
Mazeppa
Monody on the Death of the Right Hon. R. B. Sheridan
The Morgante Maggiore (A transcription project)
My Boy Hobbie O
My Epitaph
My Soul is Dark

N

Napoleon's Farewell
Napoleon's Snuff-box
The New Vicar of Bray
Newstead Abbey

O

An Occasional Prologue
Ode from the French
Ode on Venice
Ode to a Lady Whose Lover was Killed by a Ball, Which at the Same Time Shivered a Portrait Next His Heart
Ode to Napoleon Buonaparte
An Ode to the Framers of the Frame Bill
Oh! Snatched Away in Beauty's Bloom
Oh! Weep for Those
On a Change of Masters at a Great Public School
On a Cornelian Heart Which Was Broken
On a Distant View of the Village and School of Harrow on the Hill, 1806
On a Royal Visit to the Vaults (Windsor Poetics)
On Being Asked What Was the "Origin of Love"
On Finding a Fan
On Jordan's Banks
On Leaving Newstead Abbey
On Lord Thurlow's Poems
On Moore's Last Operatic Farce, or Farcical Opera
On My Thirty-third Birthday
On My Wedding-Day
On Napoleon's Escape from Elba
On Parting
On Revisiting Harrow
On Sam Rogers (same as "Lord Byron's Verses on Sam Rogers")
On the Birth of John William Rizzo Hoppner
On the Bust of Helen by Canova

On the Day of the Destruction of Jerusalem by Titus
On the Death of — Thyrza (same as "To Thyrza")
On the Death of a Young Lady
On the Death of Mr. Fox
On the Death of the Duke of Dorset
On the Eyes of Miss A— H—
On the Quotation
On the Star of "the Legion of Honour"
On this Day I complete my Thirty-sixth Year
One Struggle More, and I Am Free
Oscar of Alva
Ossian's Address to the Sun in "Carthon"

P

Parenthetical Address
Parisina
Pignus Amoris
The Prayer of Nature
The Prisoner of Chillon
The Prophecy of Dante, a Poem

Q

Quem Deus Vult Perdere Prius Dementat
Queries to Casuists

R

R. C. Dallas
Remember Him, whom Passion's Power
Remember Thee! Remember thee!
Remembrance
Remind Me Not, Remind Me Not
Reply to Some Verses of J. M. B. Pigot, Esq., on the Cruelty of his Mistress

S

Sardanapalus, a Tragedy (A transcription project)
Saul
She Walks in Beauty
The Siege of Corinth
A Sketch From Life
So We'll Go No More A-Roving
Soliloquy of a Bard in the Country
Sonetto di Vittorelli
Song (Breeze of the Night in Gentler Sighs)
Song (Fill the Goblet Again! For I Never Before)
Song (Maid of Athens, Ere We Part) (same as "Maid of Athens, Ere We Part")
Song (Thou Art Not False, But Thou Art fickle) same as "Thou Art Not False, But Thou Art Fickle")
Song (When I Roved a Young Highlander) (same as "When I Roved a Young Highlander")
Song For the Luddites
Song of Saul Before His Last Battle
Song To the Suliotes
Sonnet On Chillon

Sonnet on the Nuptials of the Marquis Antonio Cavalli with the Countess Clelia Rasponi of Ravenna

Sonnet, to Genevra (Thine eyes' Blue Tenderness, Thy Long Fair Hair)

Sonnet, to Generva (Thy Cheek is Pale with Thought, but Not From Woe). aka "Sonnet, to the Same"

Sonnet to Lake Leman

Sonnet to the Prince Regent

The Spell is Broke, the Charm is Flown!

A Spirit Passed Before Me

Stanzas (And Thou Art Dead, as Young and Fair)

Stanzas (And Wilt Thou Weep When I am Low?) (same as "And Wilt Thou Weep When I Am Low?")

Stanzas (Away, Away, Ye Notes of Woe)

Stanzas (Chill and Mirk is the Nightly Blast) (same as "Stanzas Composed During a Thunderstorm")

Stanzas (Could Love For Ever)

Stanzas (I Would I Were a Careless Child) (same as "I Would I Were a Careless Child")

Stanzas (If Sometimes in the Haunts of Men)

Stanzas (One Struggle More, and I Am Free)

Stanzas (Remember Him, Whom Passion's Power)

Stanzas (Thou Art Not False, but Thou Art Fickle)

Stanzas (Through Cloudless Skies, in Silvery Sheen) (same as "Stanzas Written in Passing the Ambracian Gulf")

Stanzas (When a Man Hath No Freedom to Fight For at Home)

Stanzas Composed During a Thunderstorm

Stanzas For Music (Bright Be the Place of Thy Soul!)

Stanzas For Music (I Speak Not, I Trace Not, I Breathe Not Thy Name)

Stanzas For Music (There Be None of Beauty's Daughters)

Stanzas For Music (There's Not a Joy the World Can Give Like That it Takes Away)

Stanzas For Music (They Say That Hope is Happiness)

Stanzas To — (same as "Stanzas to Augusta": Though the Day of My Destiny's Over)

Stanzas To a Hindoo Air

Stanzas To a Lady, on Leaving England

Stanzas To a Lady, with the Poems of Camoëns

Stanzas To Augusta (When all around grew drear and dark)

Stanzas To Augusta (Though the day of my Destiny's over)

Stanzas To Jessy

Stanzas To the Po

Stanzas To the Same (same as "There was a Time, I need not name")

Stanzas Written in Passing the Ambracian Gulf

Stanzas Written on the Road Between Florence and Pisa

Substitute For an Epitaph

Sun of the Sleepless!

Sympathetic Address to a Young Lady (same as "Lines to a Lady Weeping")

T

The Tear

There Be None of Beauty's Daughters (see "Stanzas for Music")

There Was a Time, I Need Not Name

There's Not a Joy the World Can Give Like That it Takes Away (see "Stanzas for Music")

They say that Hope is Happiness (see "Stanzas for Music")

Thou Art Not False, but Thou Art Fickle

Thou Whose Spell Can Raise the Dead (same as "Saul")

Thoughts Suggested by a College Examination

Thy Days are Done

To — (But Once I Dared to Lift My Eyes)
To — (Oh! Well I Know Your Subtle Sex)
To A— (same as "To M—")
To a Beautiful Quaker
To a Knot of Ungenerous Critics
To a Lady (Oh! Had My Fate Been Join'd with Thine)
To a Lady (This Band, Which Bound Thy yellow Hair)
To a Lady (When Man, Expell'd from Eden's Bowers)
To a Lady Weeping (same as "Lines To a Lady Weeping")
To a Lady who Presented to the Author a Lock of Hair Braided with His Own, and Appointed a Night in December to Meet Him in the Garden
To a Vain Lady
To a Youthful Friend
To an Oak at Newstead
To Anne (Oh, Anne, Your Offences to Me Have Been Grievous)
To Anne (Oh Say Not, Sweet Anne, That the Fates Have Decreed)
To Belshazzar
To Caroline (Oh! When Shall the Grave Hide For Ever My Sorrow?)
To Caroline (Think'st thou I saw thy beauteous eyes)
To Caroline (When I Hear you Express an Affection so Warm)
To Caroline (You Say You Love, and Yet Your Eye)
To D—
To Dives. A Fragment
To E—
To Edward Noel Long, Esq.
To Eliza
To Emma
To E. N. L. Esq. (same as "To Edward Noel Long, Esq.")
To Florence
To George Anson Byron (?)
To George, Earl Delawarr
To Harriet
To Ianthe (The "Origin of Love!"—Ah, why) (same as "On Being Asked What Was the 'Origin of Love'")
To Ianthe (from Canto I of Childe Harold's Pilgrimage) (Not in Those Climes Where I Have Late Been Straying)
To Inez (from Canto I of Childe Harold's Pilgrimage) (Nay, Smile Not at My Sullen Brow)
To Julia (same as "To Lesbia!")
To Lesbia!
To Lord Thurlow
To M—
To Maria — (same as "To Emma")
To Mrs. — (same as "Well! Thou Art Happy")
To Mrs. Musters (same as "Stanzas To a Lady, On Leaving England")
To M. S. G. (When I Dream That You Love Me, You'll Surely Forgive)
To M. S. G. (Whene'er I View Those Lips of Thine)
To Marion
To Mary, on Receiving Her Picture
To Miss E. P. (same as "To Eliza")
To Mr. Murray (For Orford and for Waldegrave)
To Mr. Murray (Strahan, Tonson, Lintot of the Times)

To Mr. Murray (To Hook the Reader, You, John Murray)
To my Son
To Penelope
To Romance
To Samuel Rogers, Esq. (same as "Lines Written On a Blank Leaf of The Pleasures of Memory")
To Sir W. D. (same as "To a Youthful Friend")
To the Author of a Sonnet
To the Countess of Blessington
To the Duke of D— (same as "To the Duke of Dorset")
To the Duke of Dorset
To the Earl of — (same as "To the Earl of Clare")
To the Earl of Clare
To the Honble. Mrs. George Lamb
To the Prince Regent on the Repeal of the Bill of Attainder Against Lord E. Fitzgerald, June, 1819.
(same as "Sonnet to the Prince Regent")
To the Rev. J. T. Becher (same as "Lines: Addressed to the Rev. J. T. Becher")
To the Same (same as "And Wilt Thou Weep When I Am Low?")
To the Sighing Strephon
To Thomas Moore (My Boat is on the Shore)
To Thomas Moore (Oh you, Who in all Names Can Tickle the Town)
To Thomas Moore (What Are You Doing Now)
To Thyrza (Without a Stone to Mark the Spot)
To Thyrza (One Struggle More, and I Am Free) (same as "One Struggle More, and I am Free")
To Time
To Woman
Translation from Anacreon Ode 1. (I Wish to Tune My Quivering Lyre)
Translation from Anacreon Ode 5. (Mingle with the Genial Bowl)
Translation from Catullus: Ad Lesbiam
Translation from Catullus: Lugete Veneres Cupidinesque
Translation from Horace
Translation from the "Medea" of Euripides [Ll. 627–660]
Translation from Vittorelli
Translation of a Romaic Love Song
Translation of the Epitaph on Virgil and Tibullus, by Domitius Marsus
Translation of the Famous Greek War Song
Translation of the Nurse's Dole in the Medea of Euripides
Translation of the Romaic Song
The Two Foscari, a Tragedy (A transcription project)

U

V

Venice. A Fragment
Verses Found in a Summer-house at Hales-Owen
Versicles
A Version of Ossian's Address to the Sun
A very Mournful Ballad on the Siege and Conquest of Alhama
Vision of Belshazzar
The Vision of Judgment (A transcription project)
A Volume of Nonsense

www.ingramcontent.com/pod-product-compliance
Lightning Source LLC
Chambersburg PA
CBHW060050050426
42448CB00011B/2379